Old Fart Adorable

Beautiful Critters with Bad Mouths

By

R. Randolph

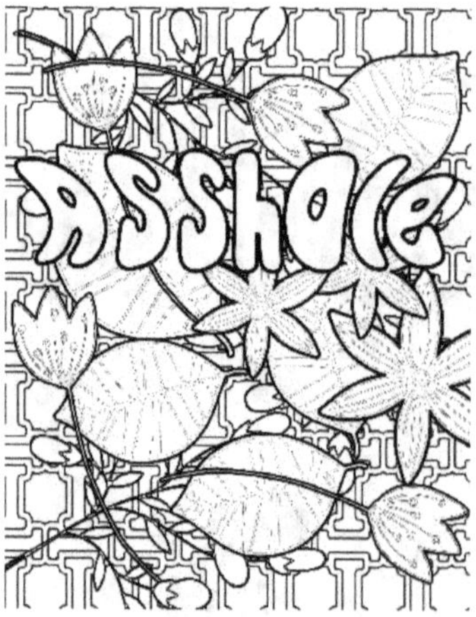

Happy Coloring!

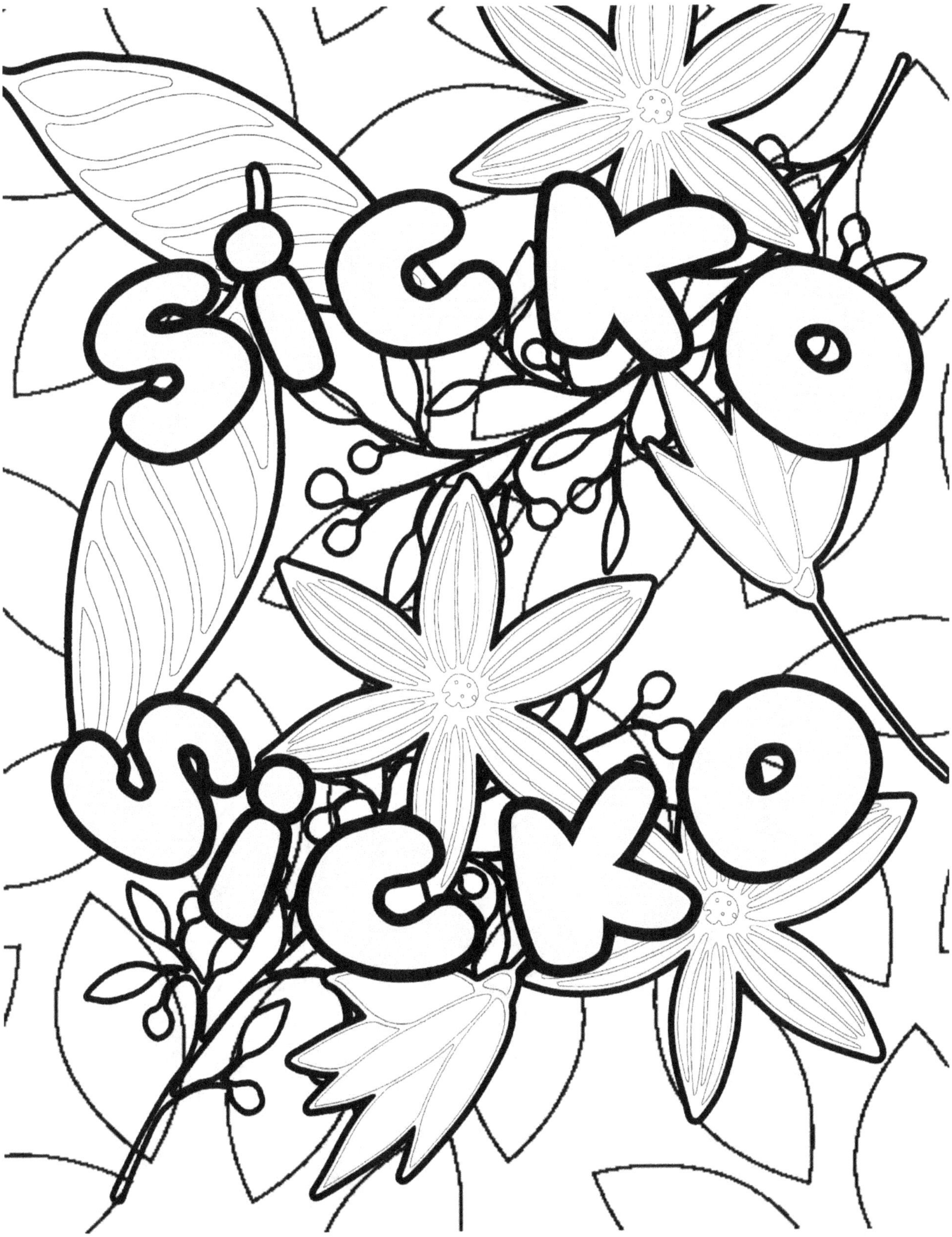
Sicko
Sicko

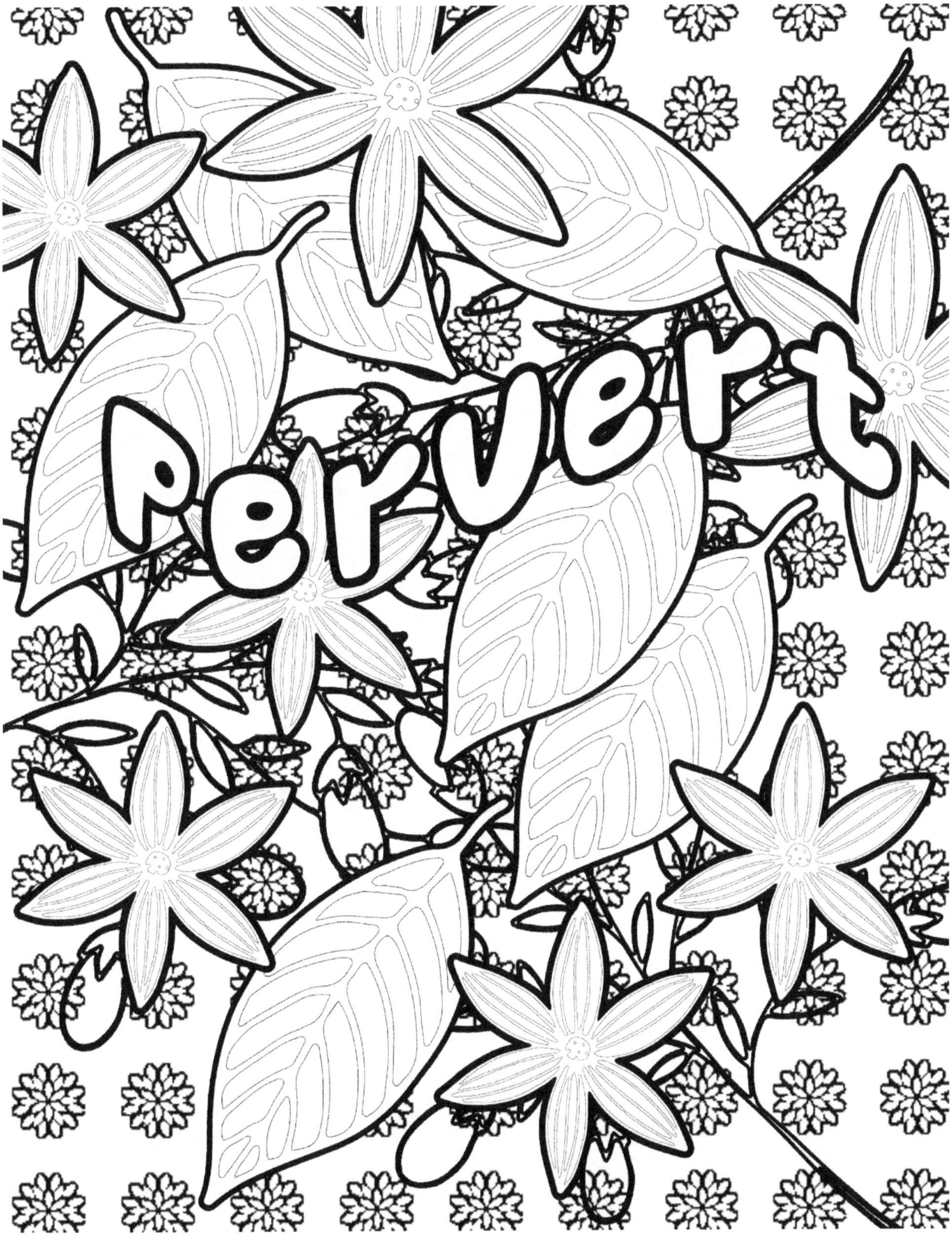
Pervert

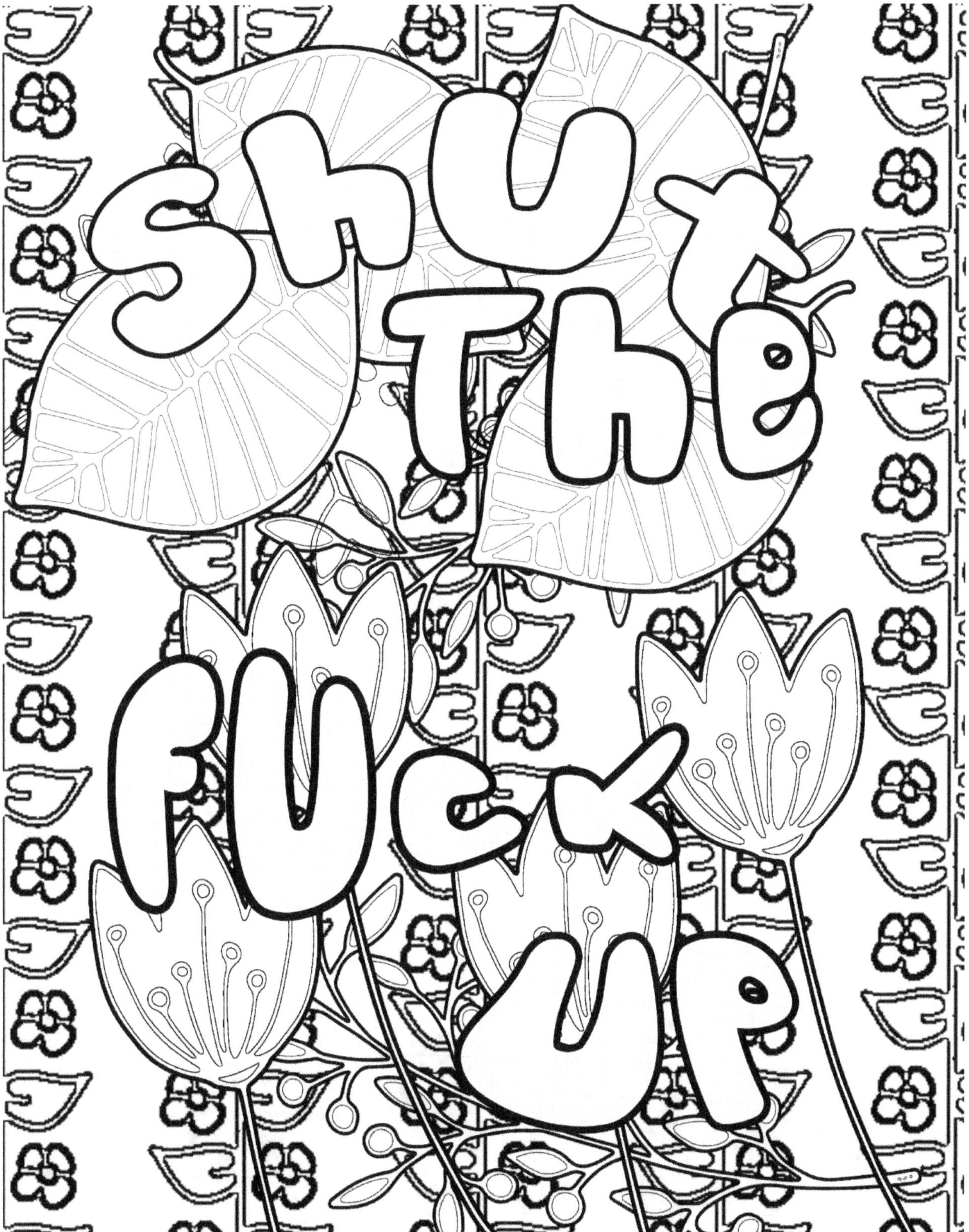
Shut The Fuck Up

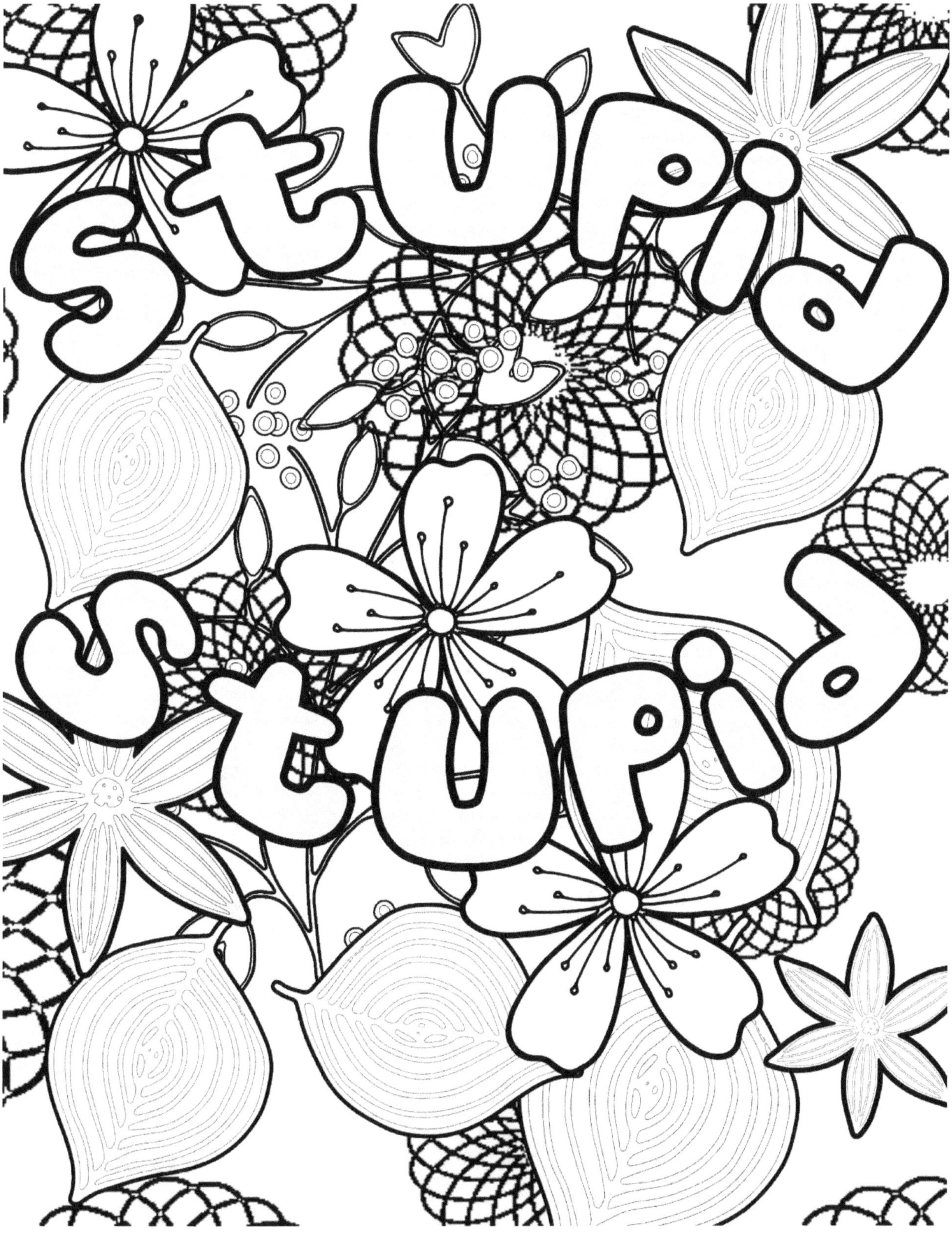
stupid
stupid

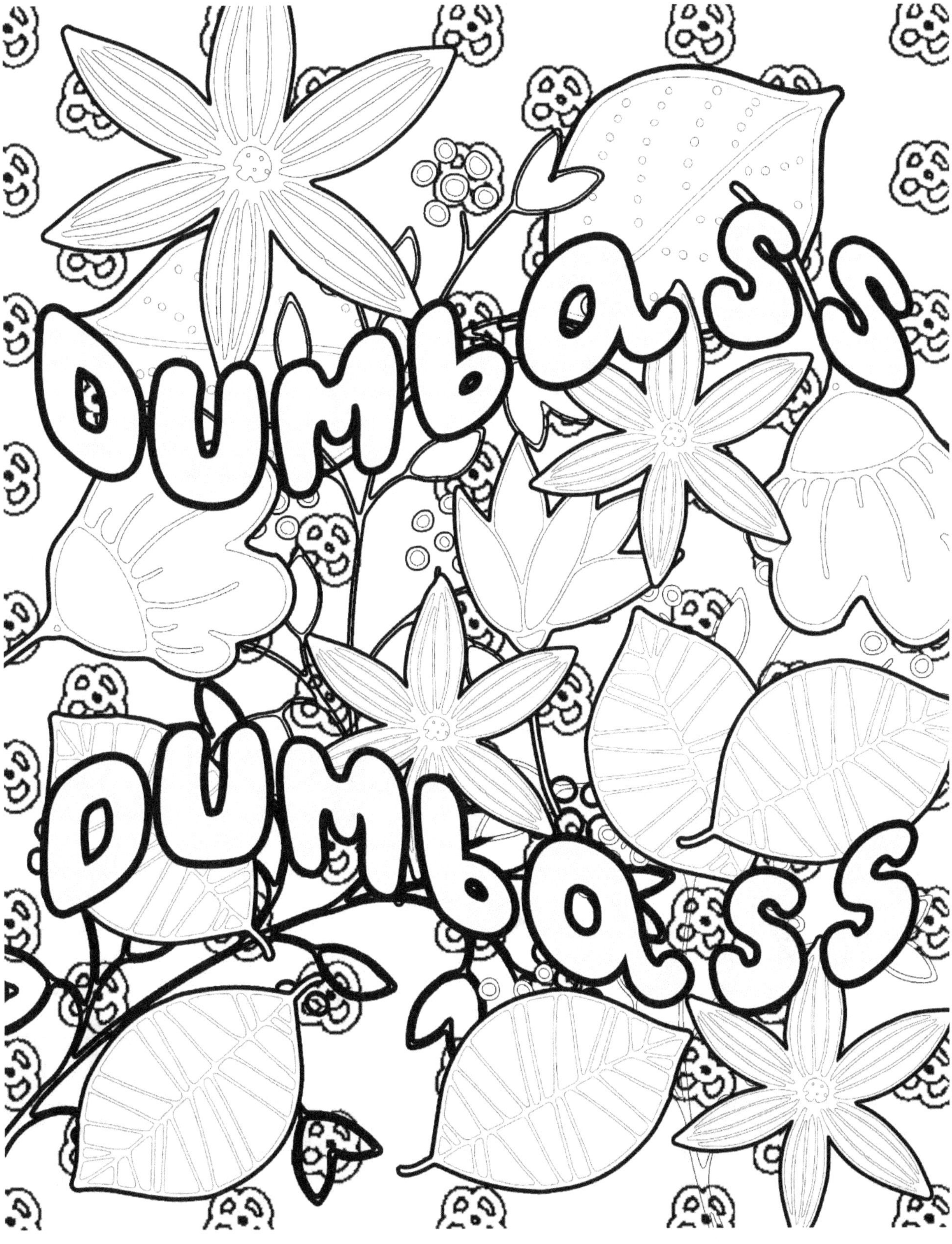
DUMBASS
DUMBASS

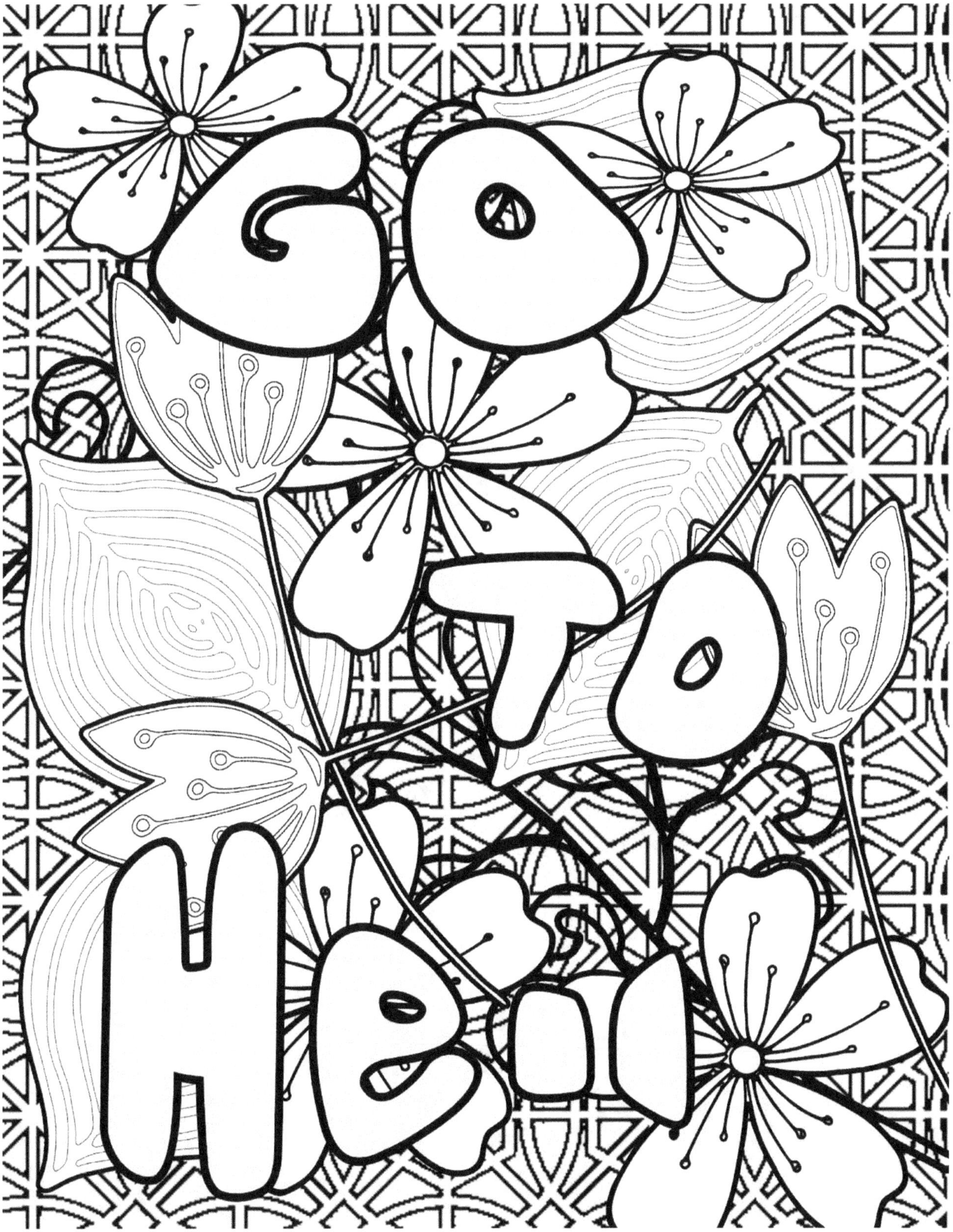
GO TO HELL

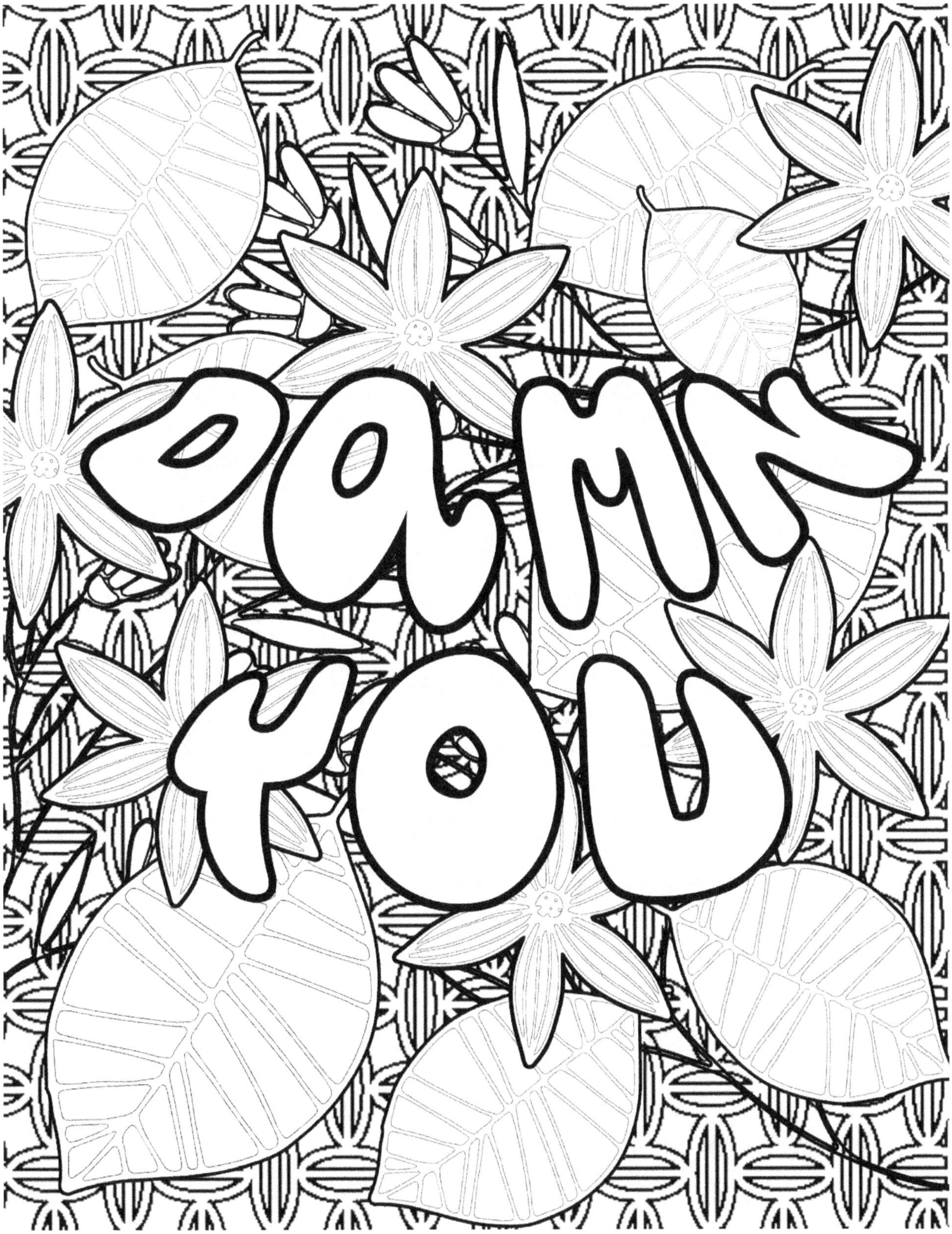
DAMN
YOU

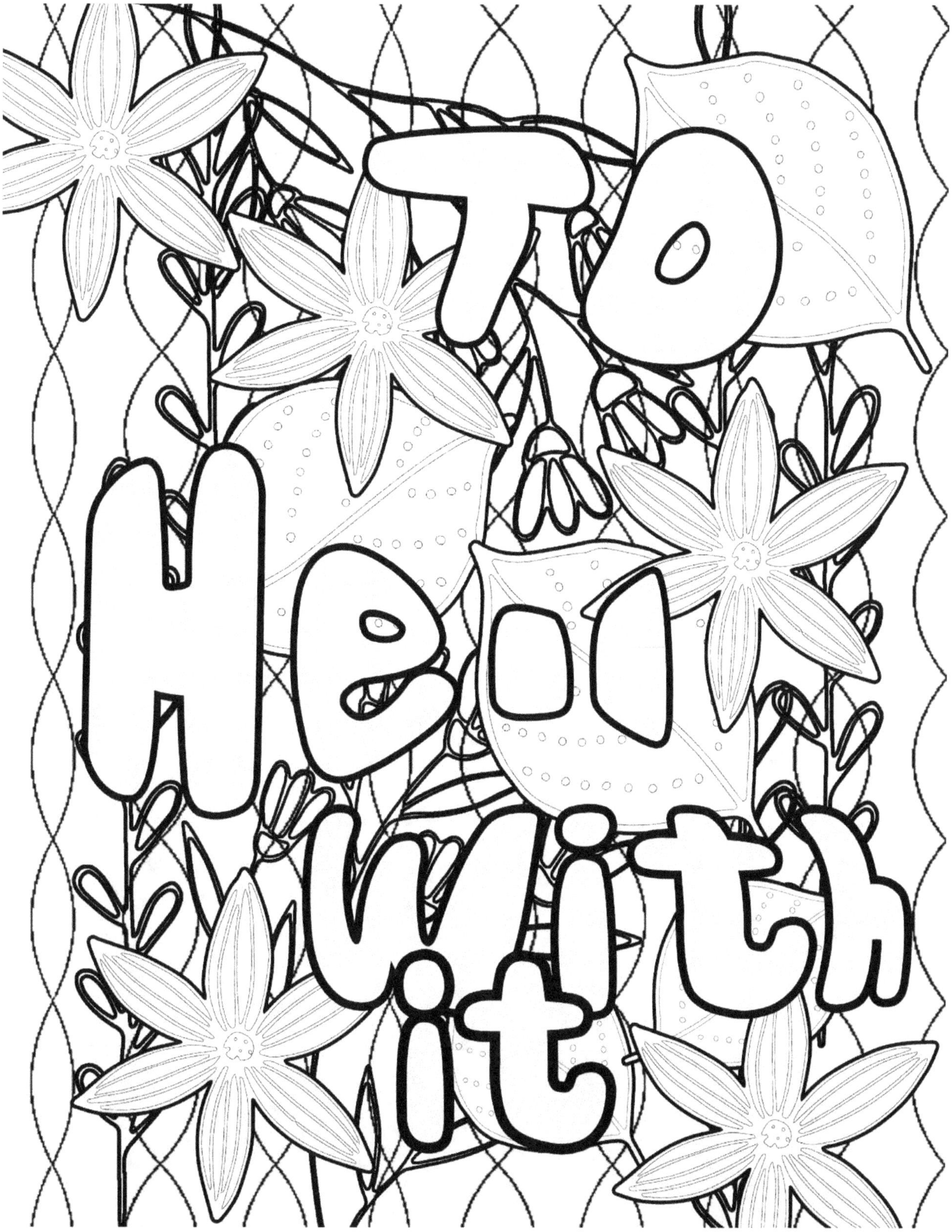
To
Hell
with
it

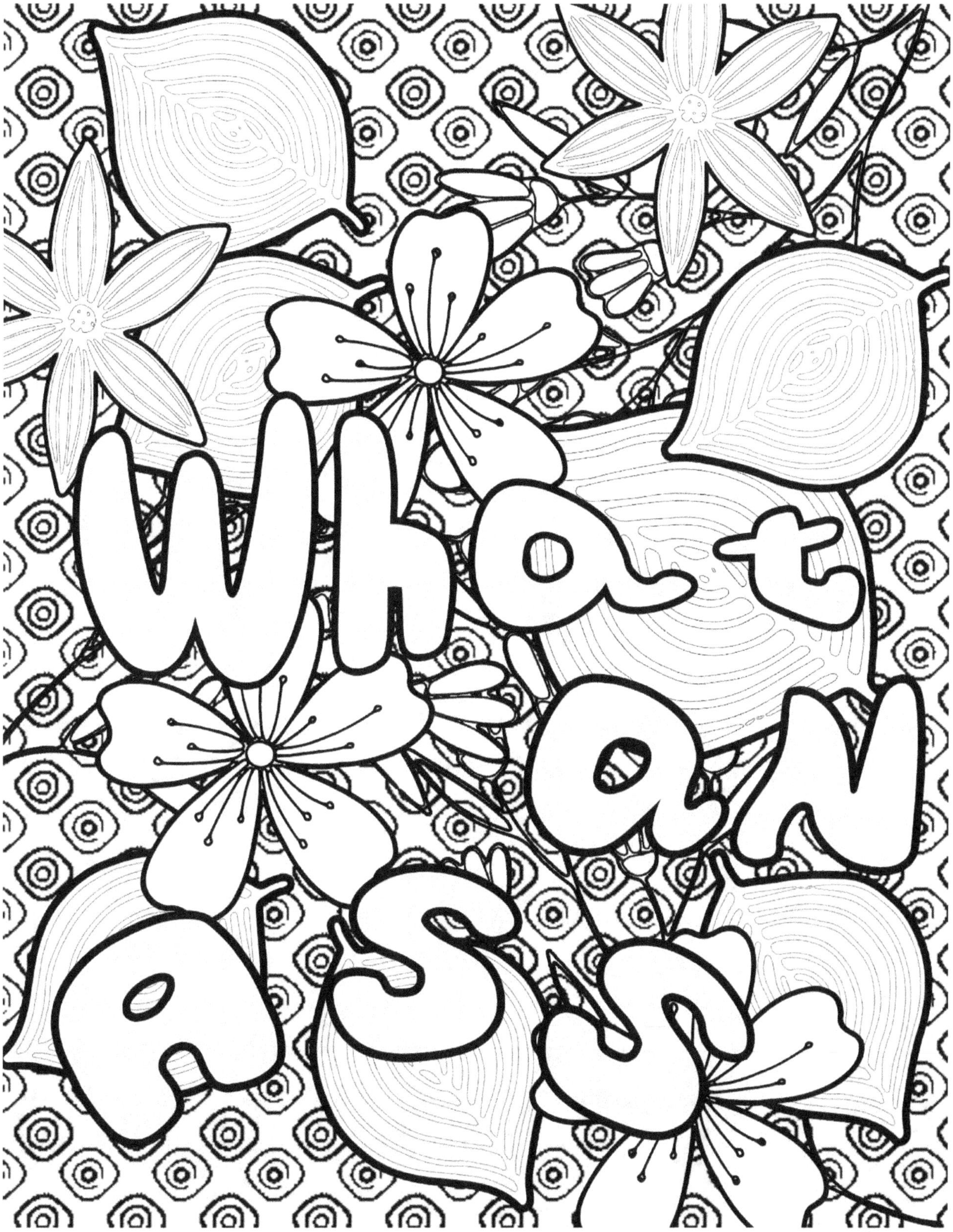
What an Ass

Bitch
Please

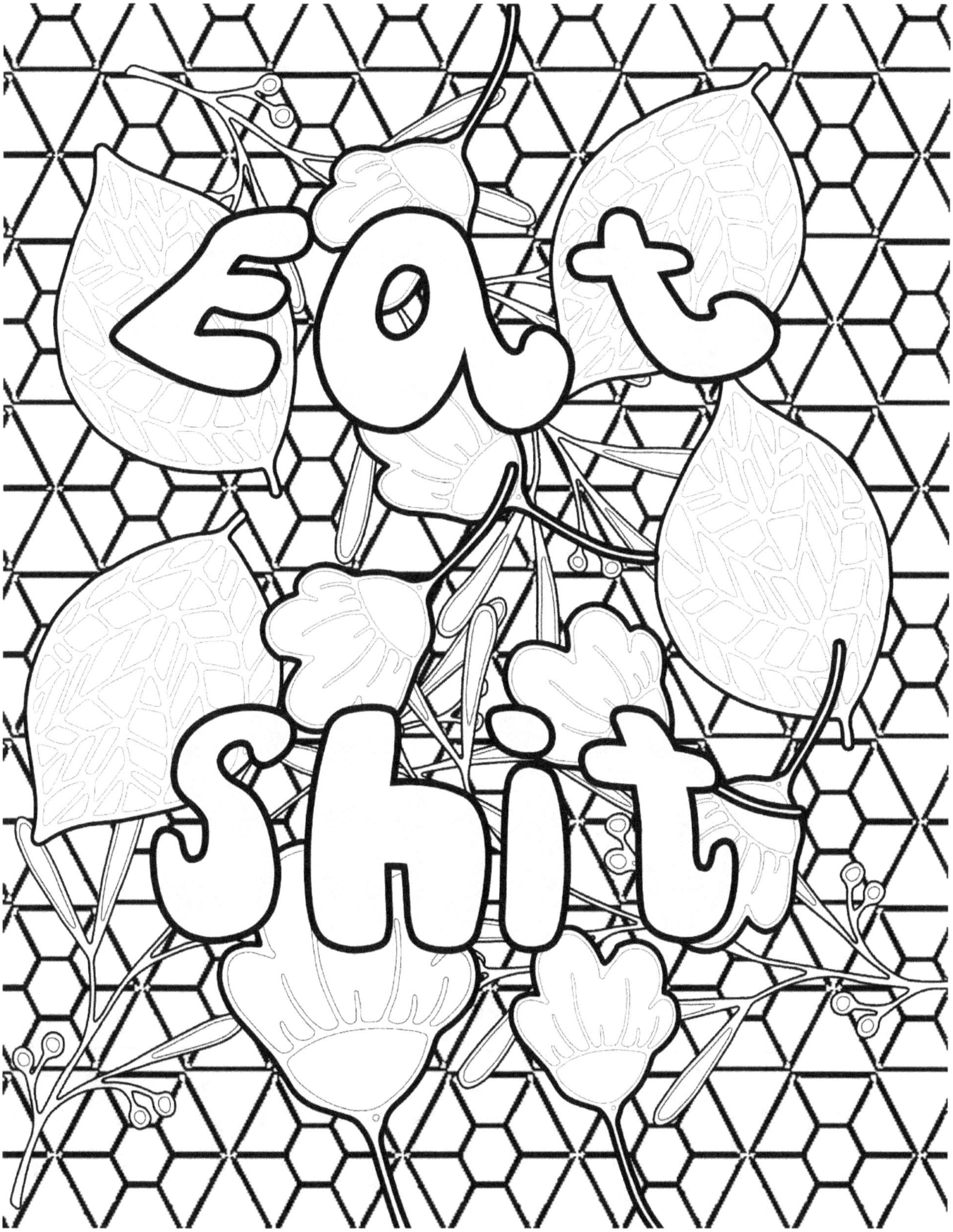
Eat
Shit

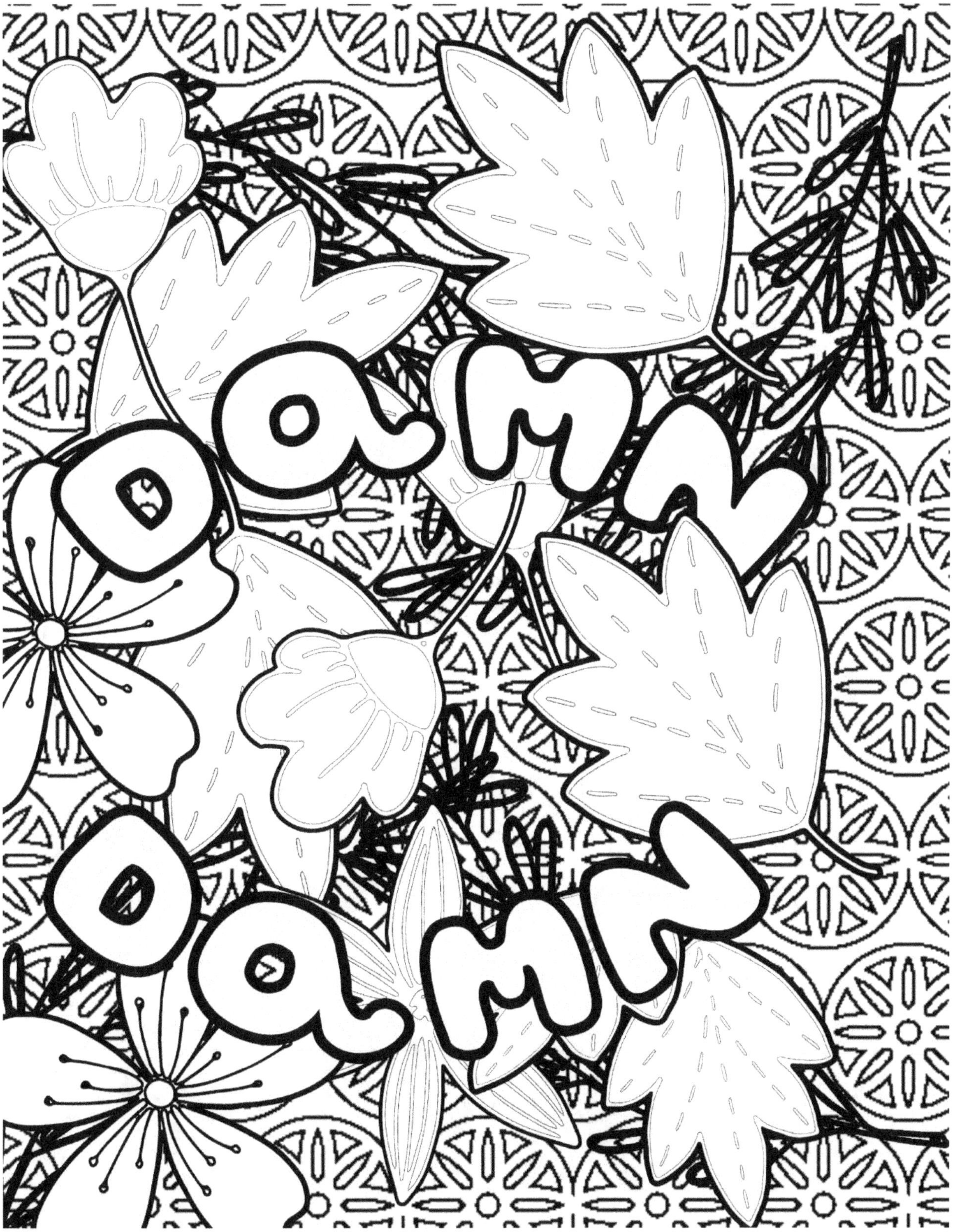
Damn
Damn

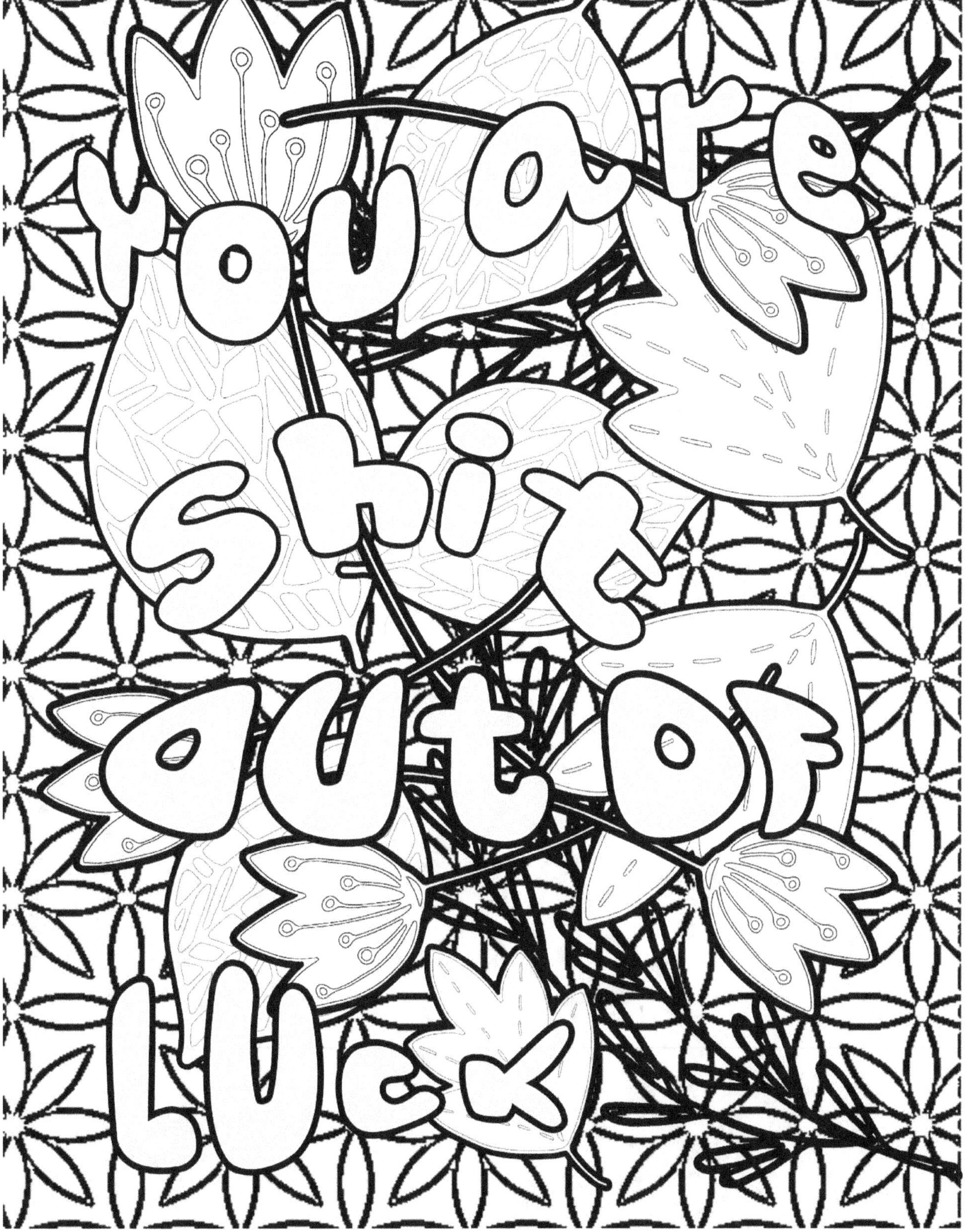
You are
Shit
out of
Luck

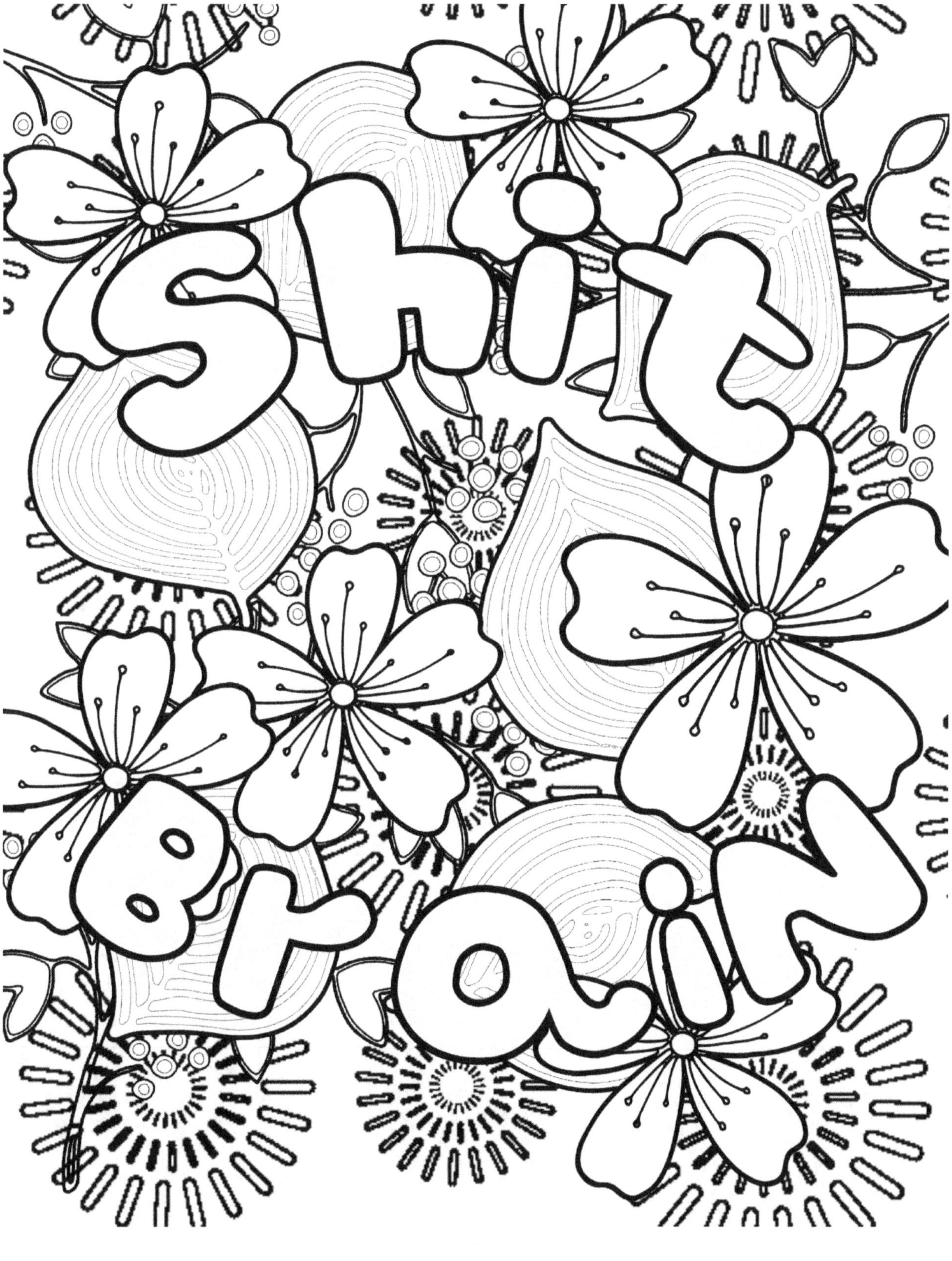
Shit
Brain

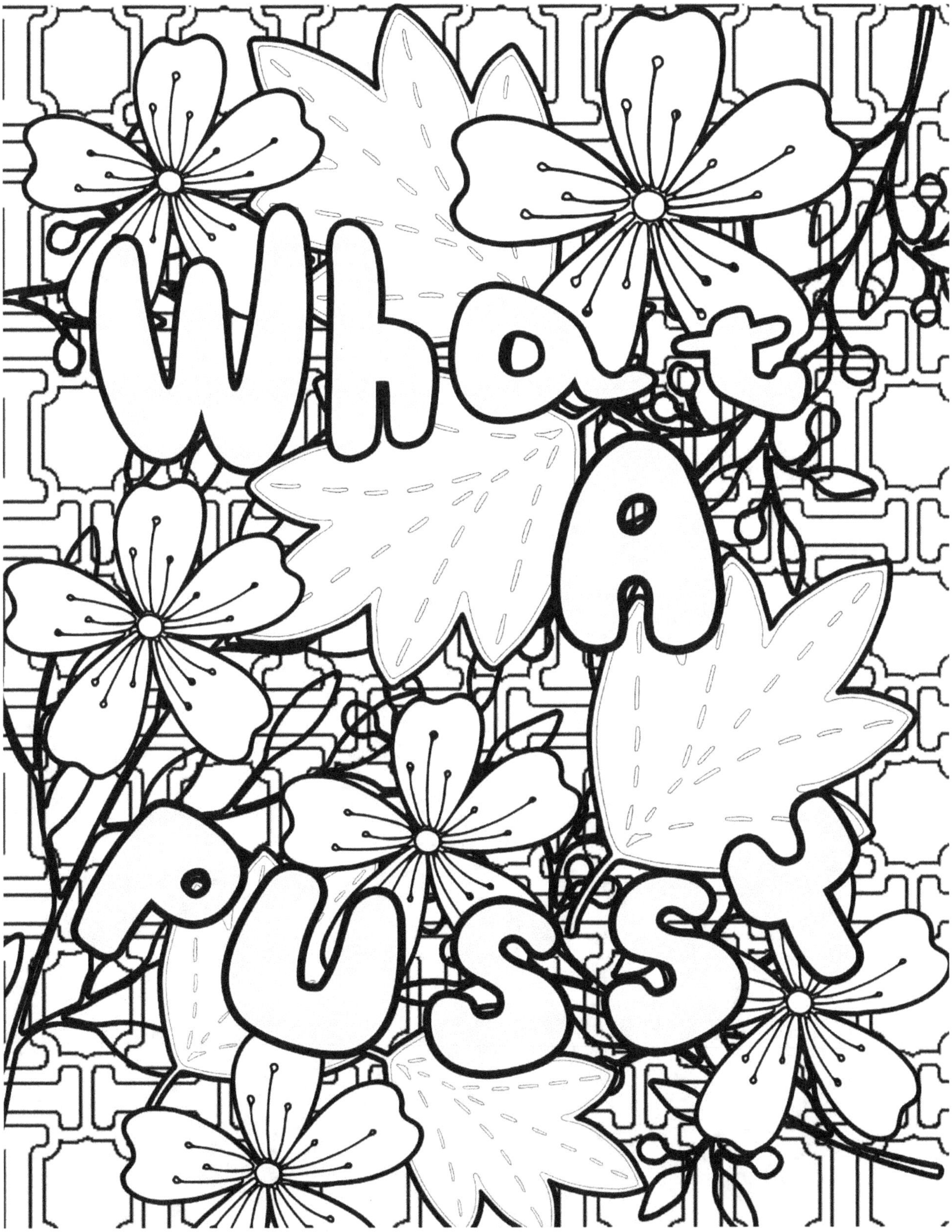
What A Pussy

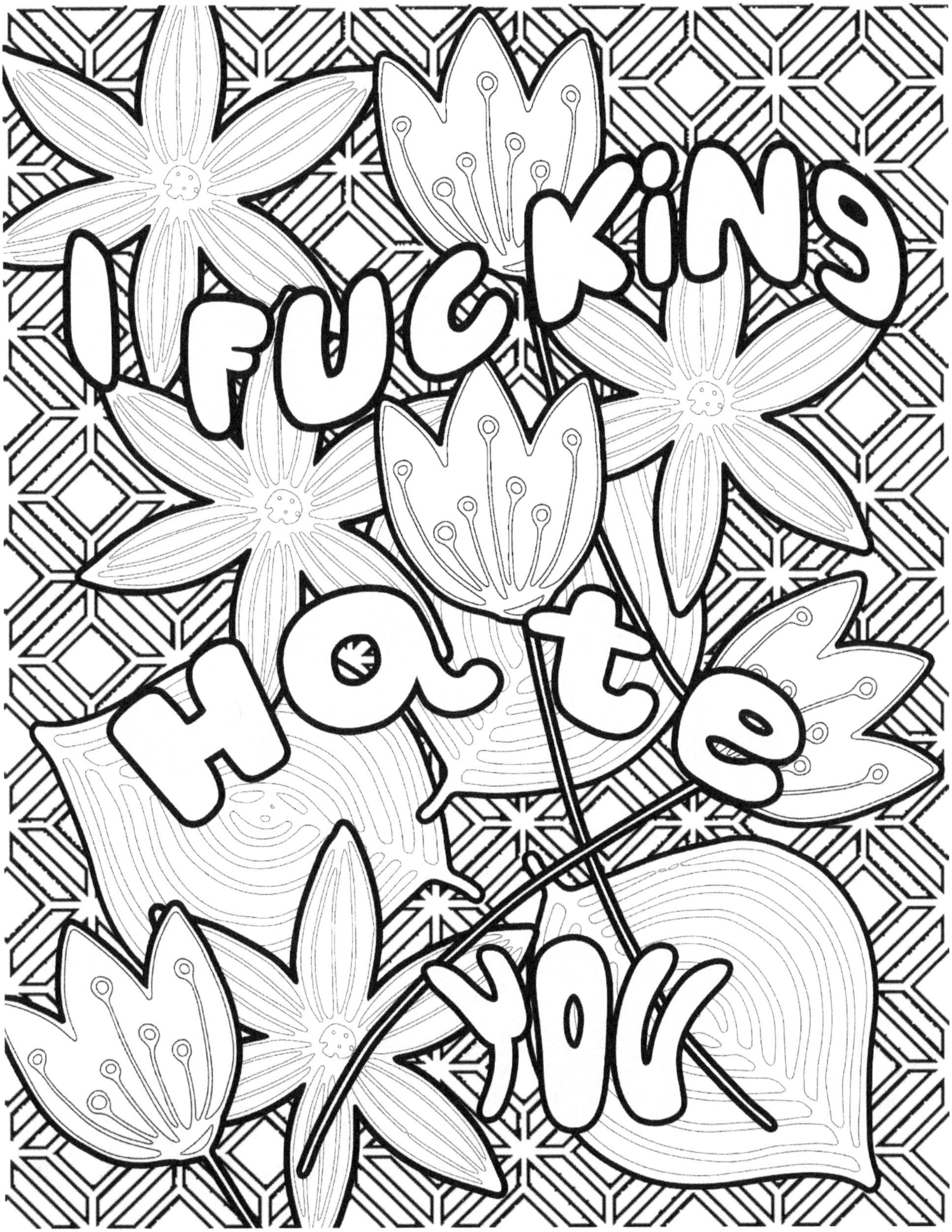
I FUCKING
HATE
YOU

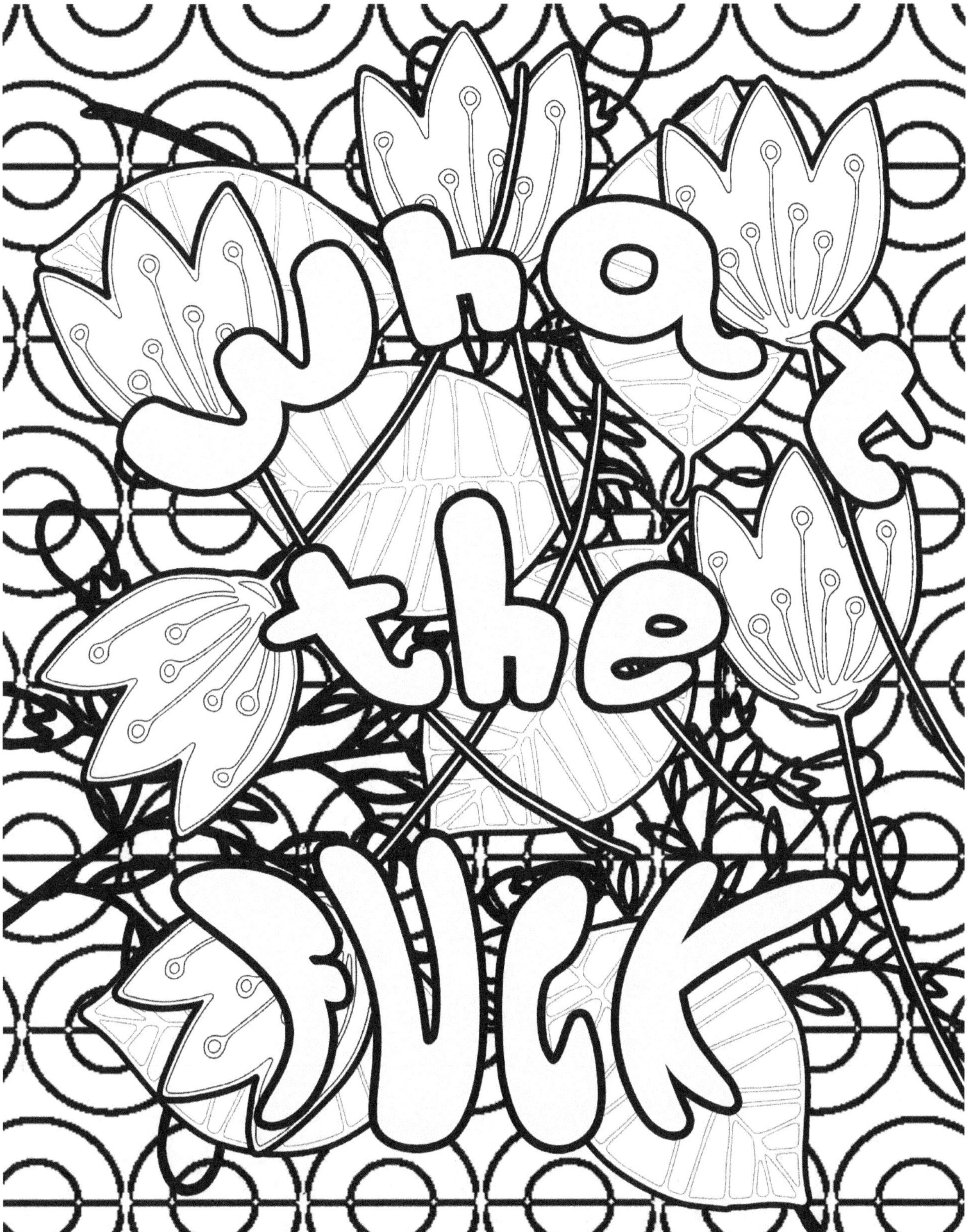
What the Fuck

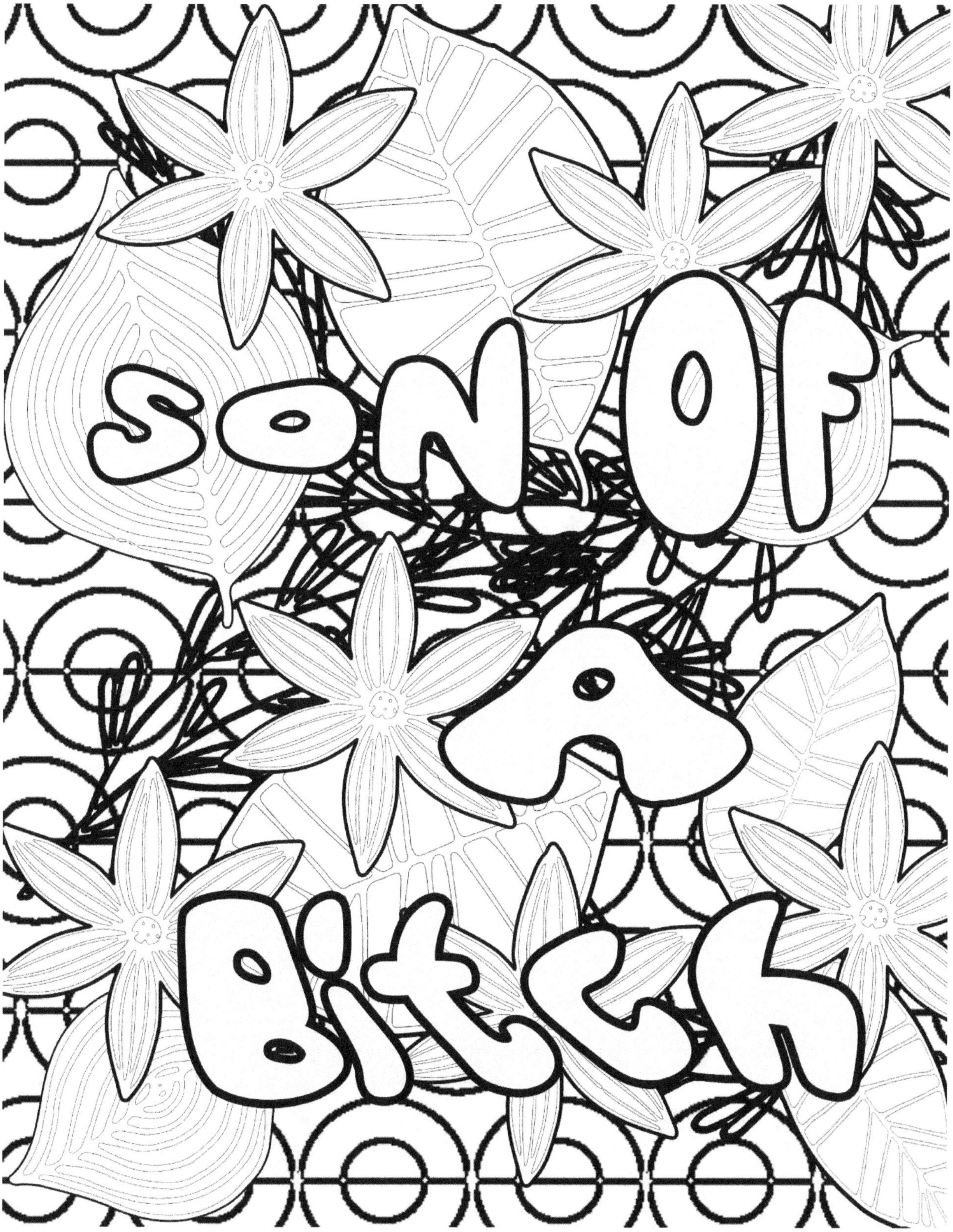
SON OF
A
BITCH

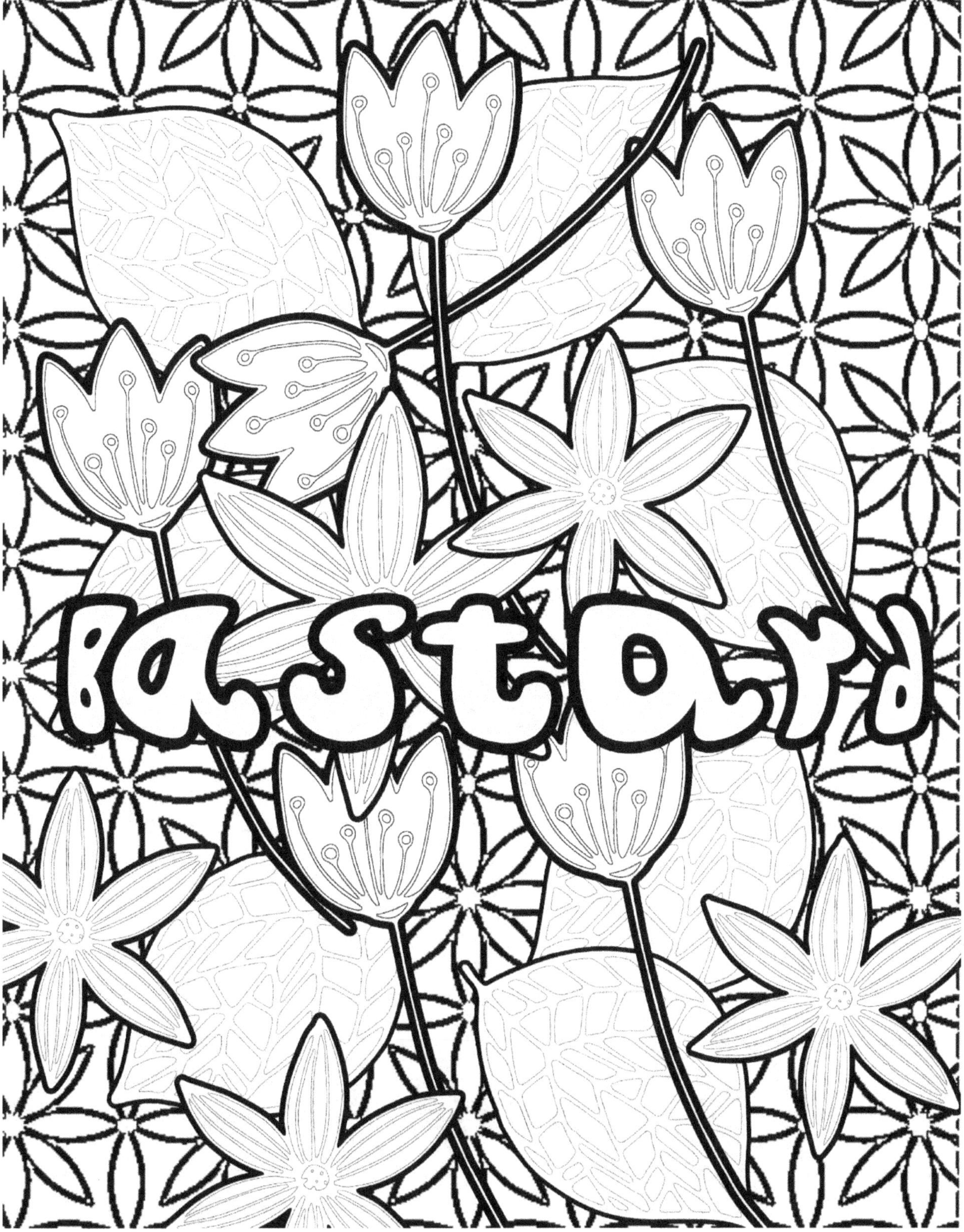
Bastard

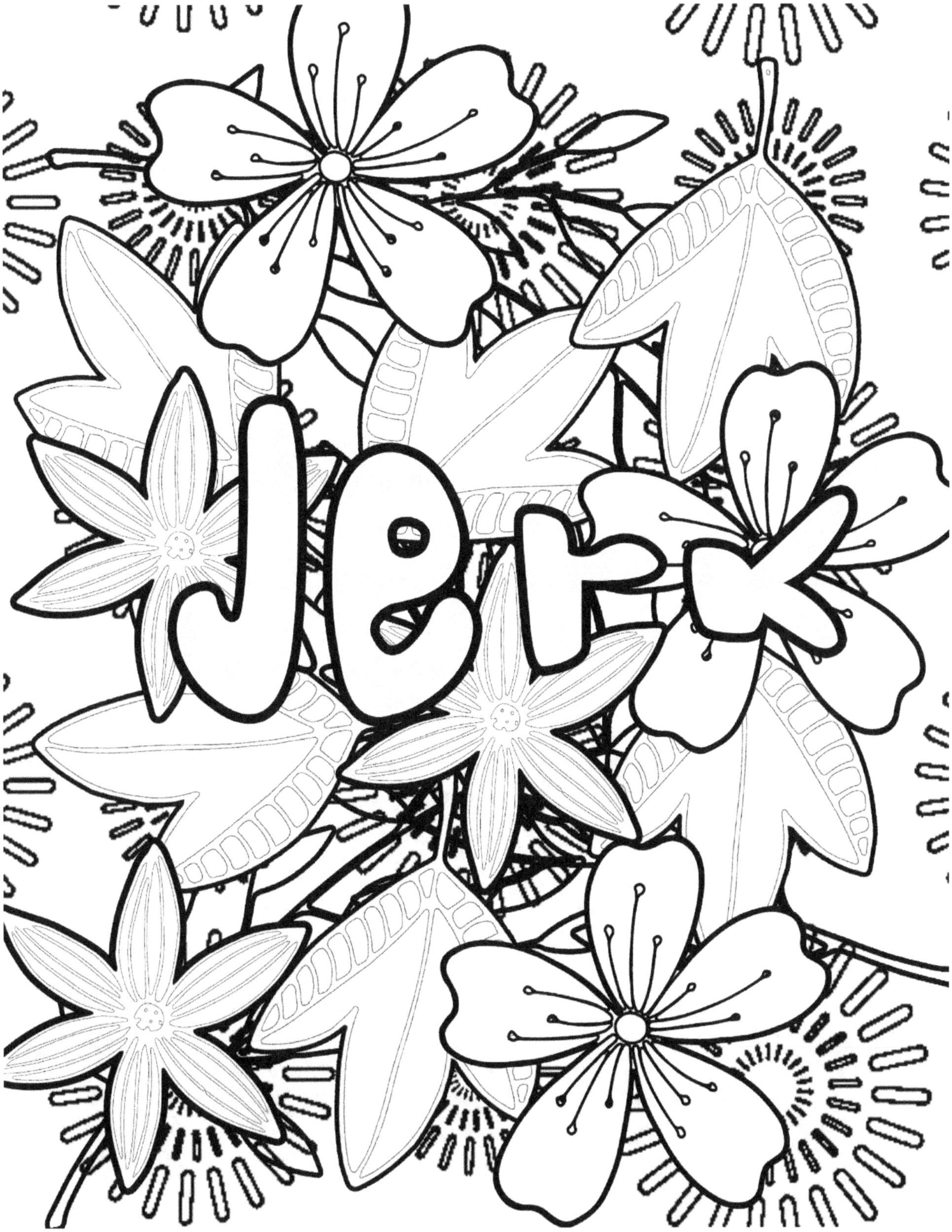
Jerk

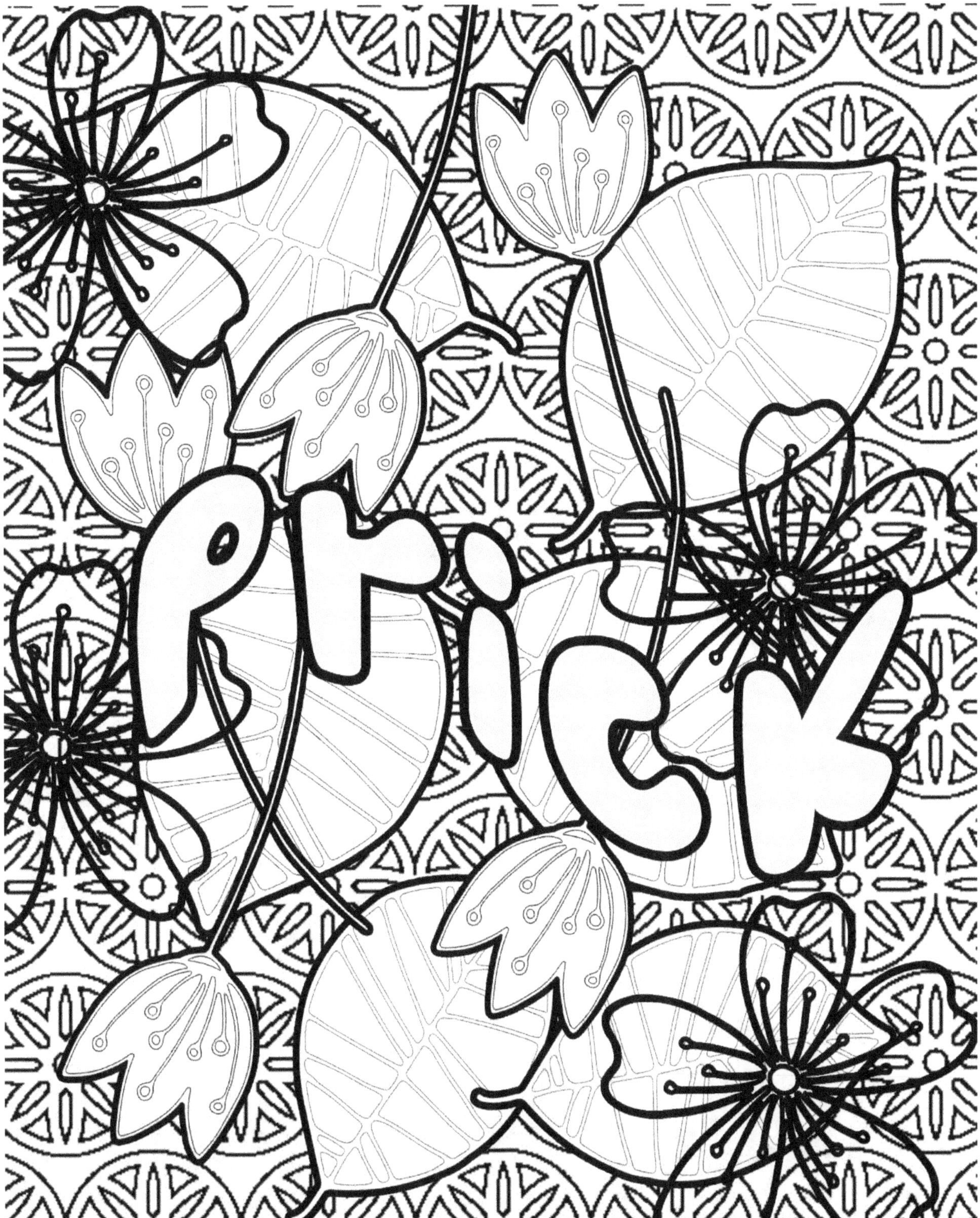
Prick

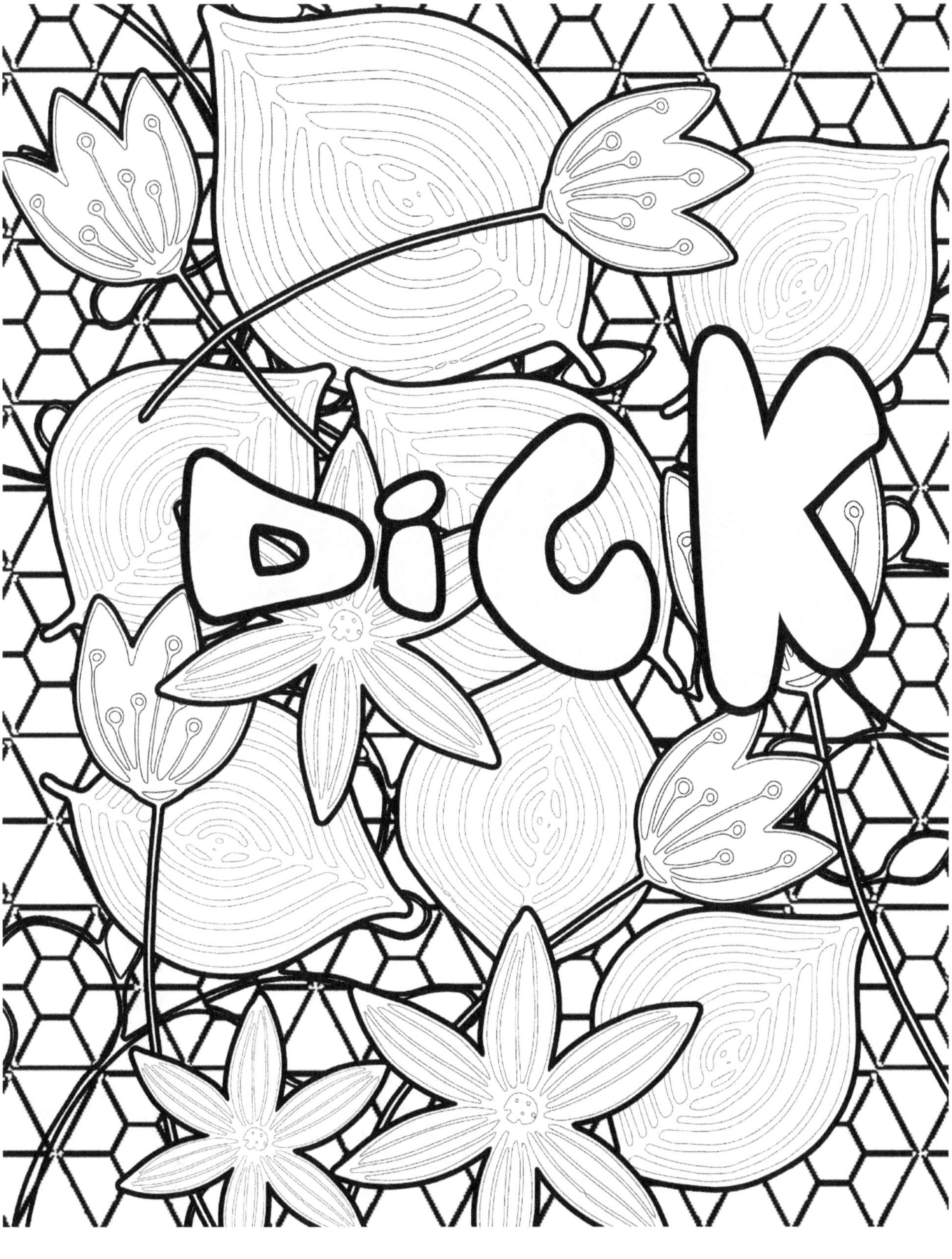
DiCK

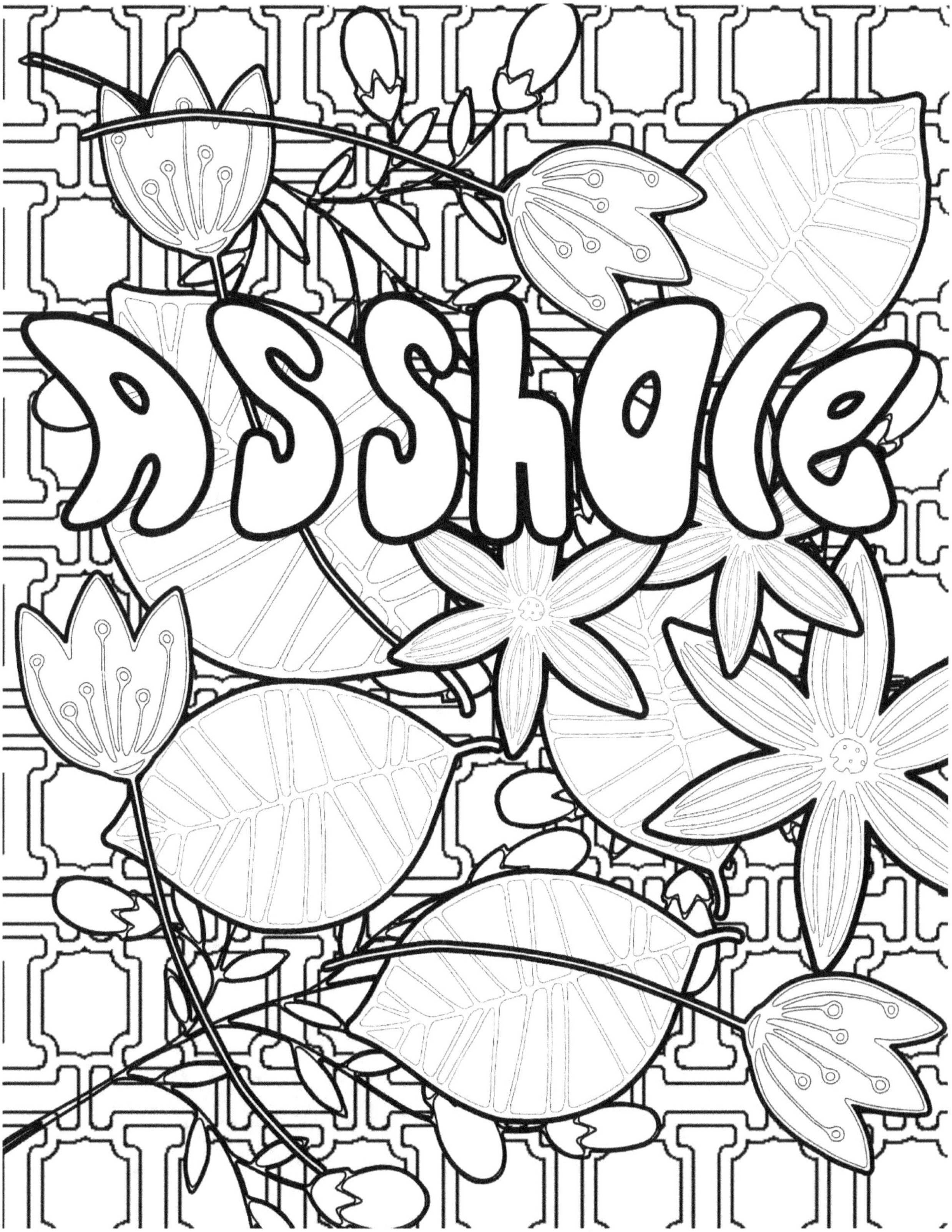
Asshole

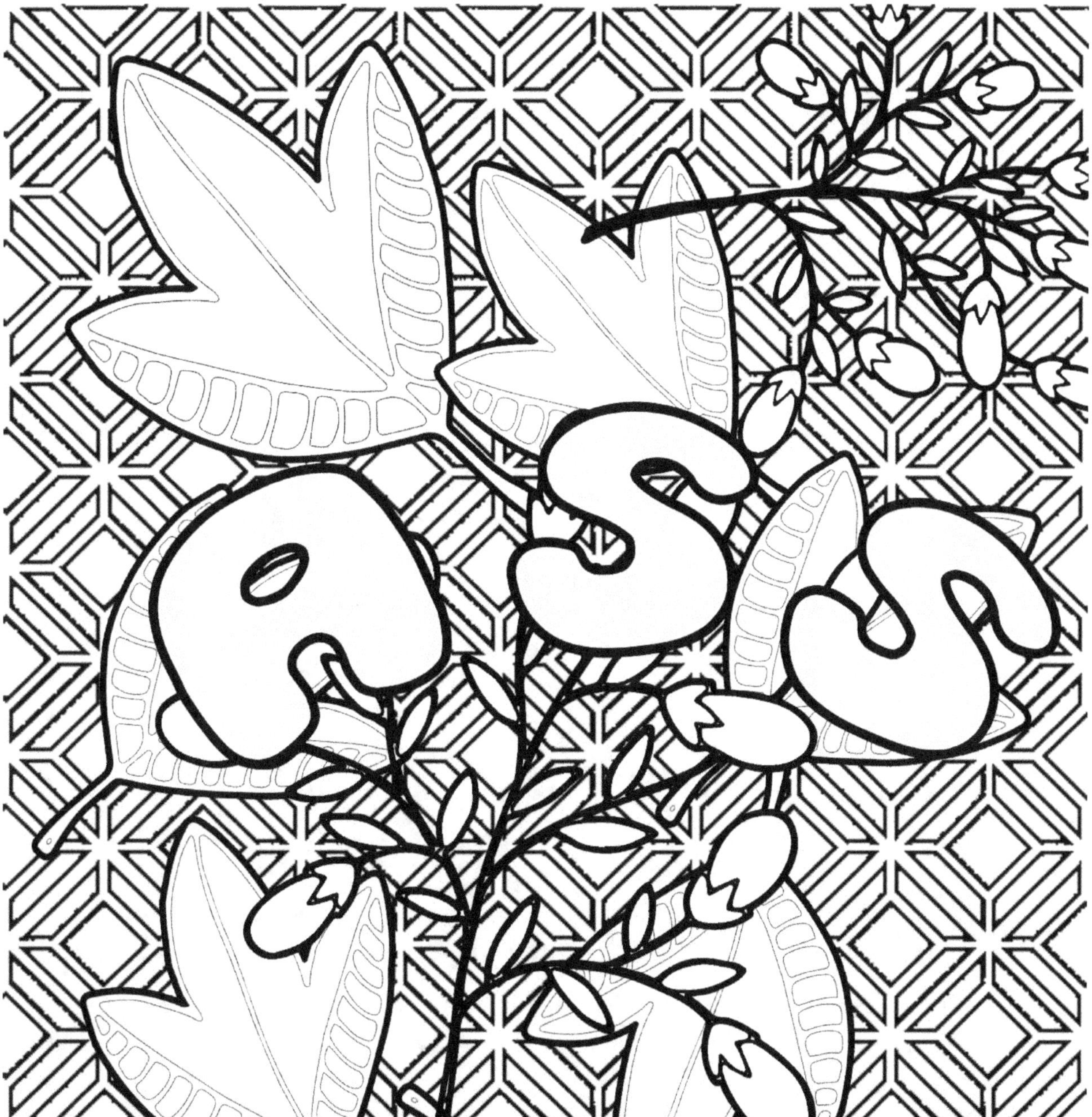
ASS

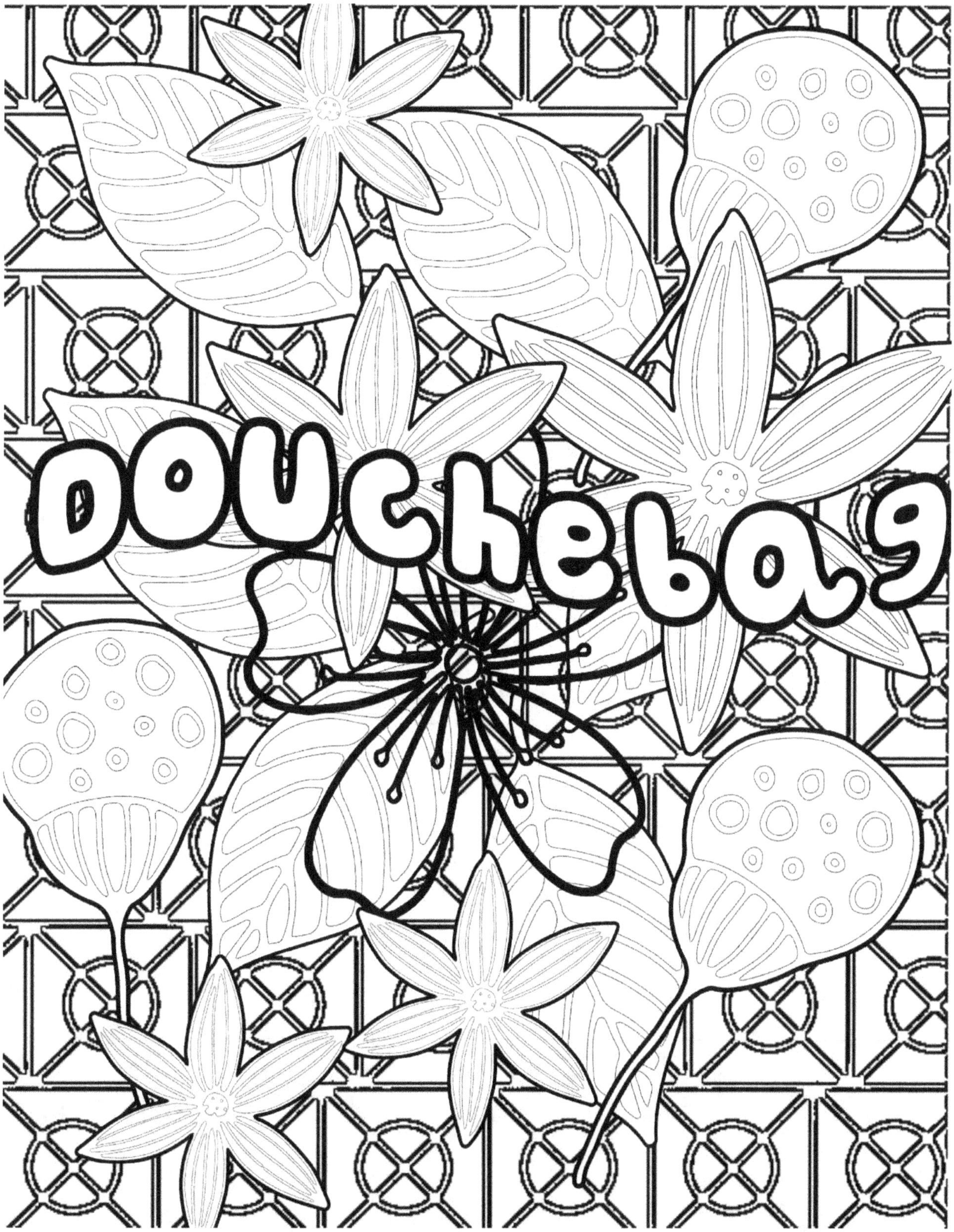
DOUChebag

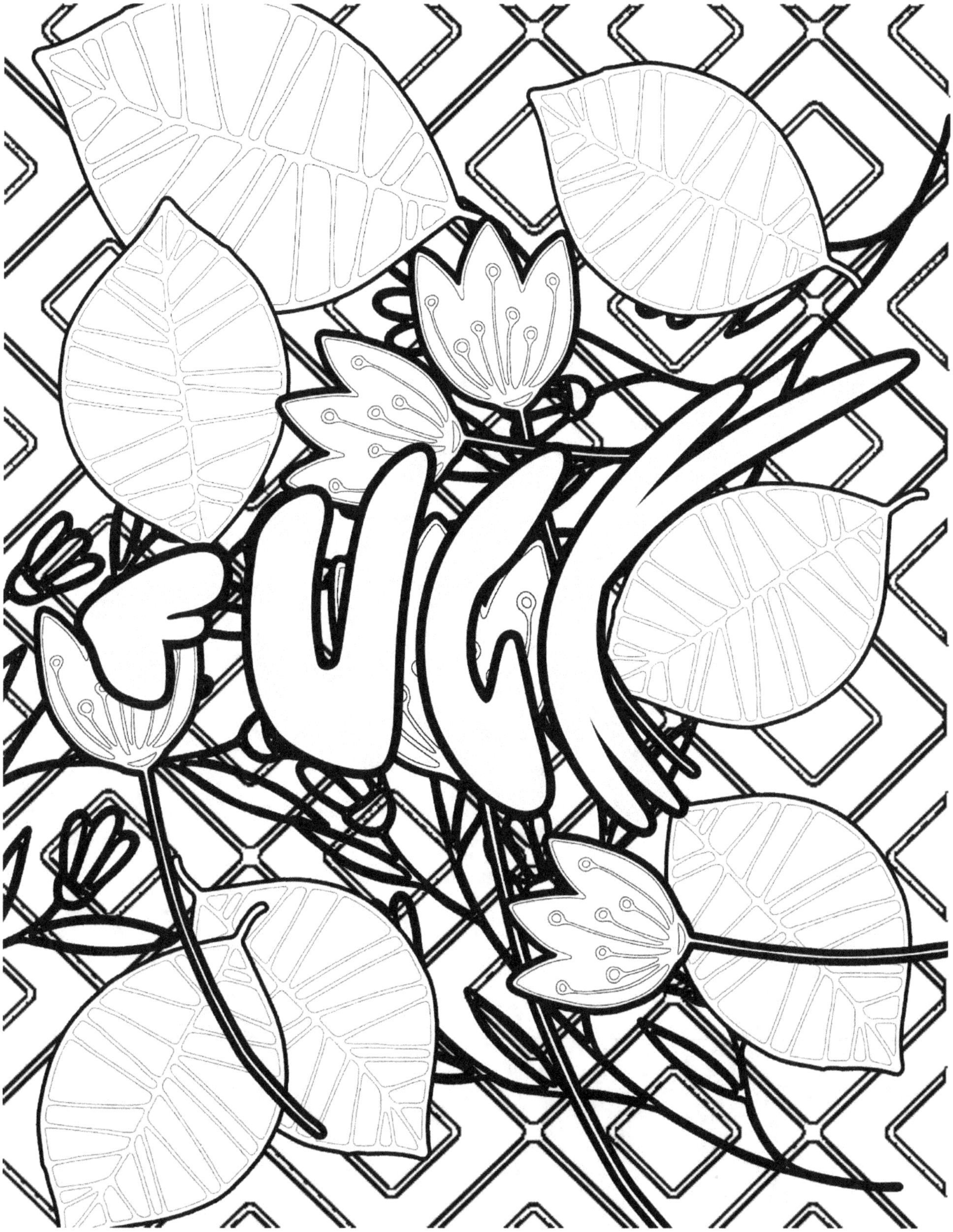
FUCK

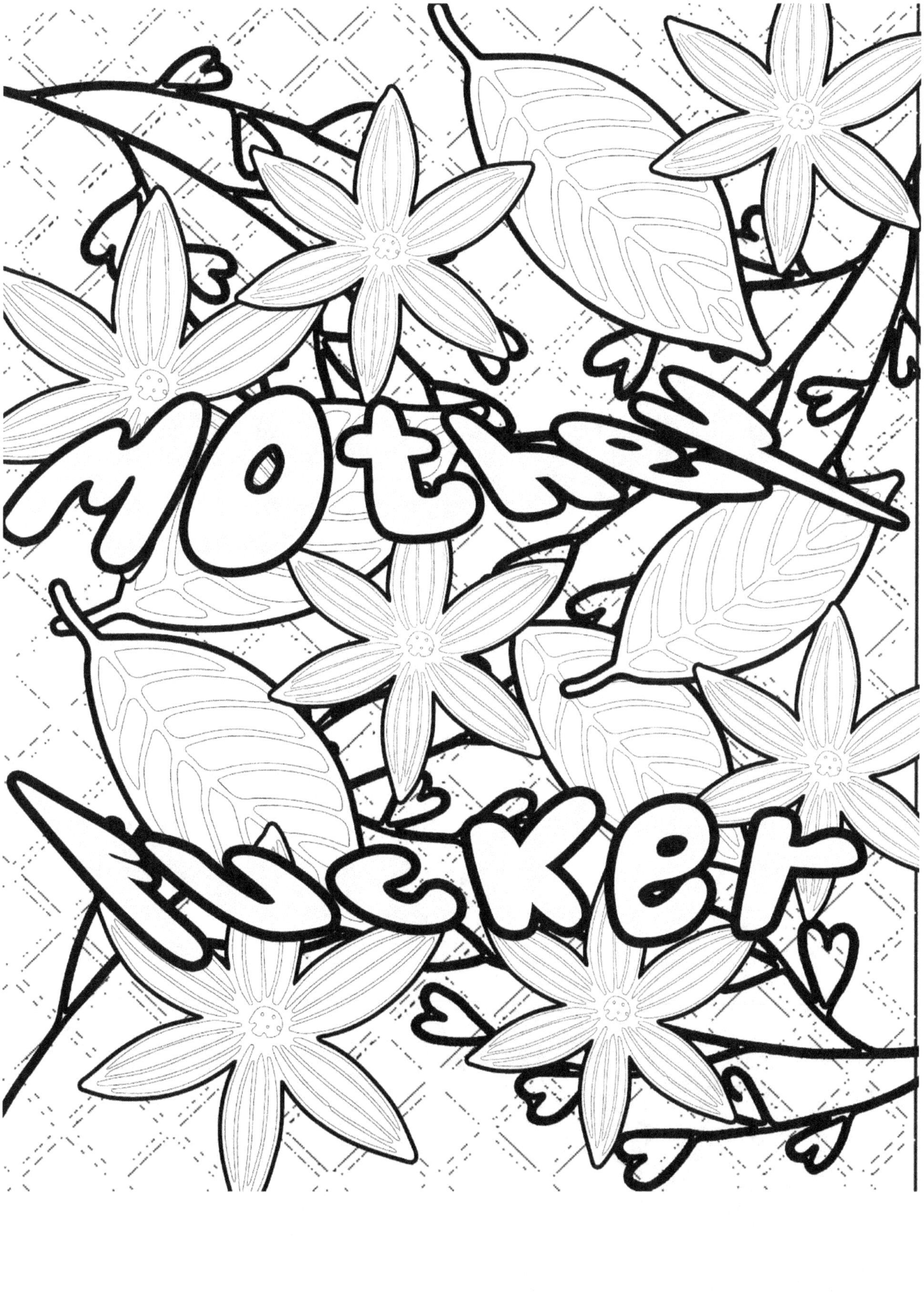
Mother
Fucker

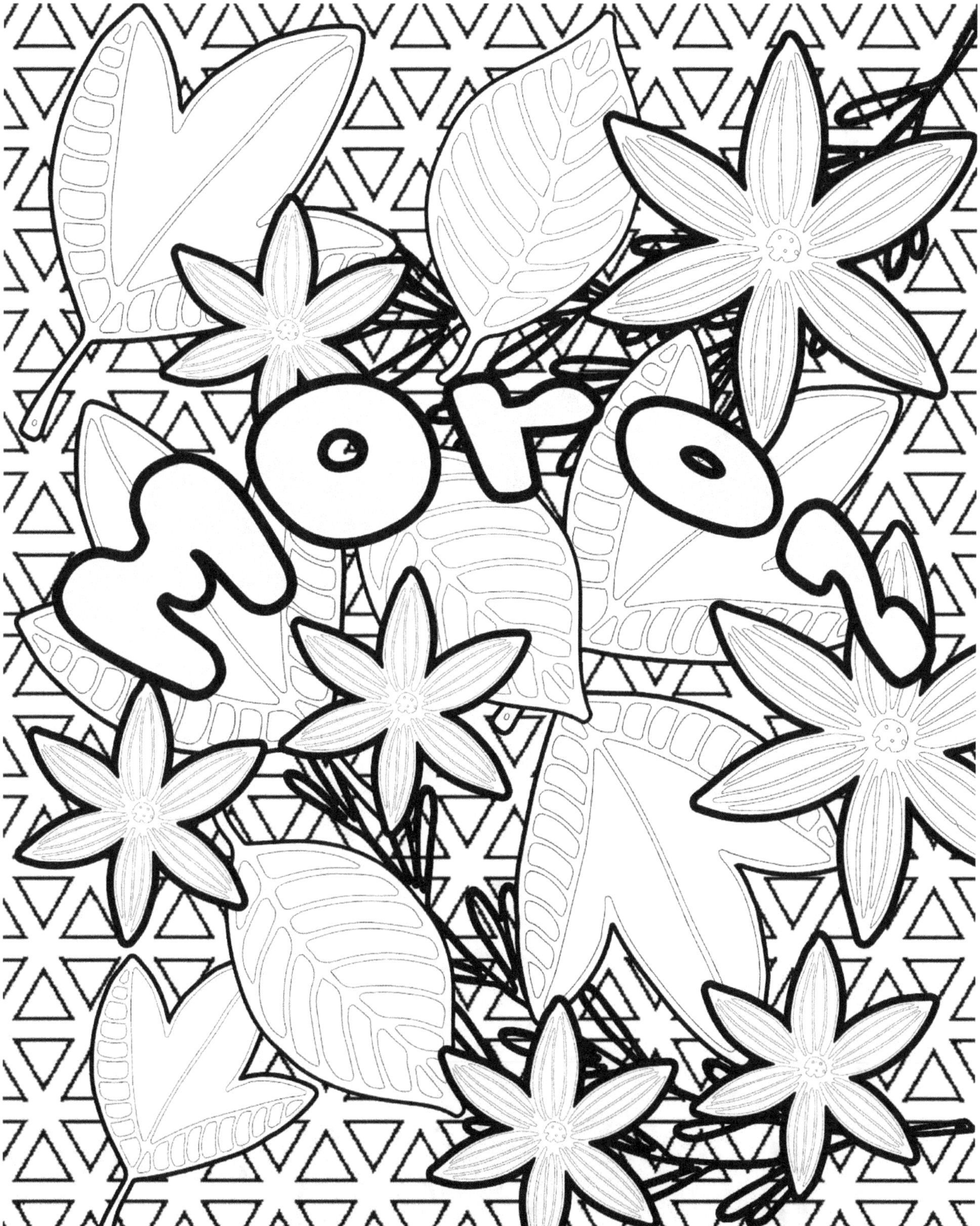
Moron

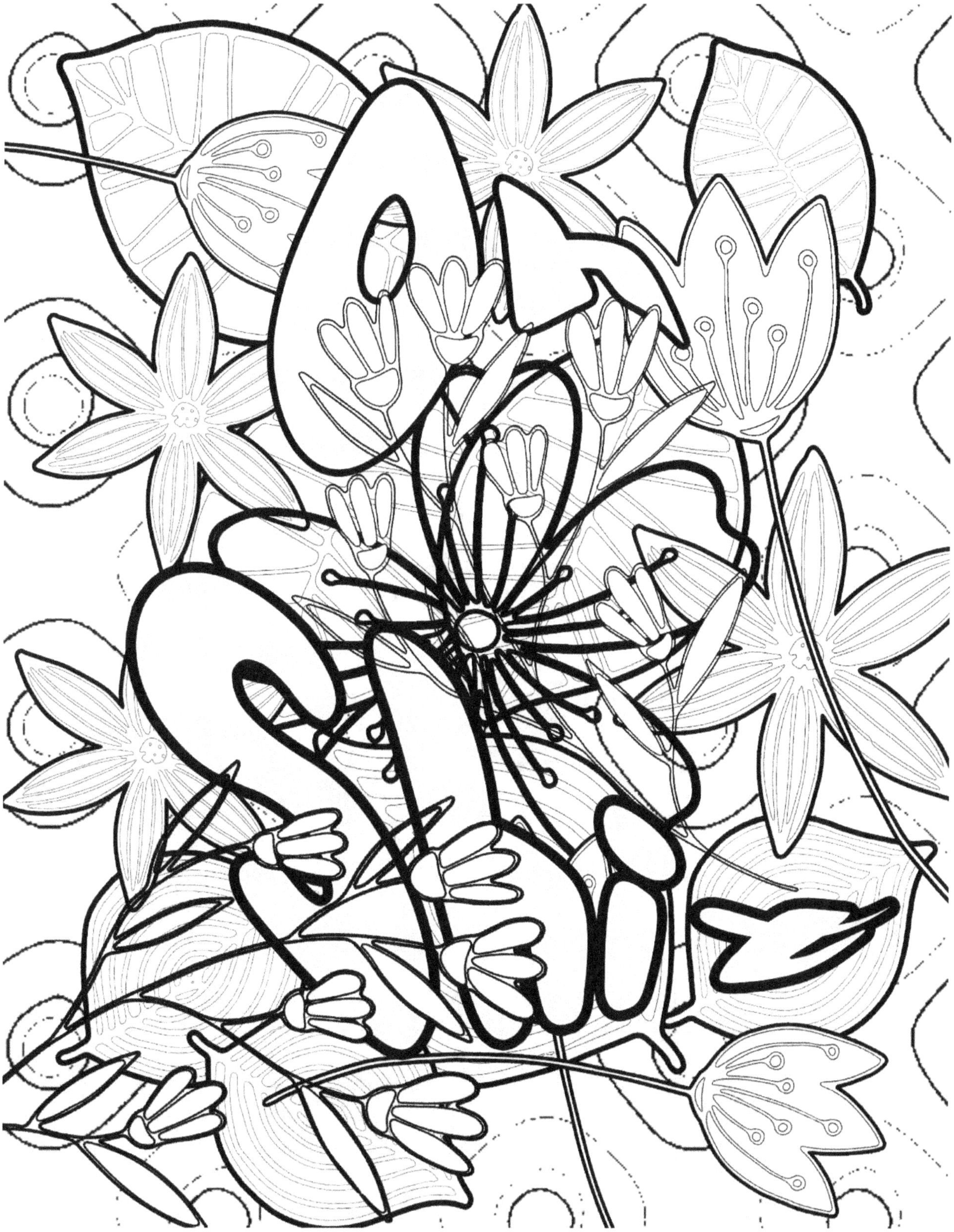
Oh Shit

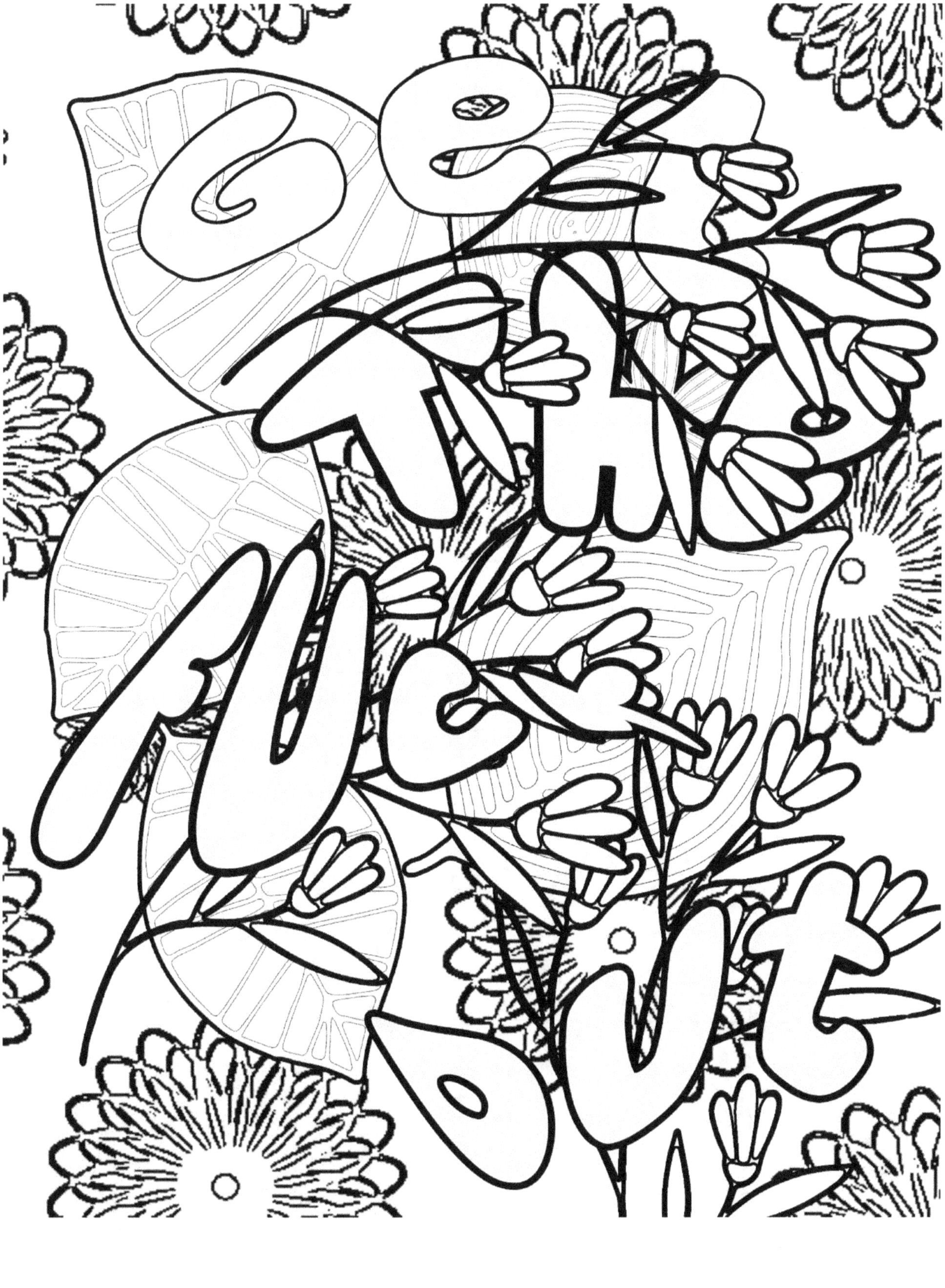
Ge
Th
Fuc
out

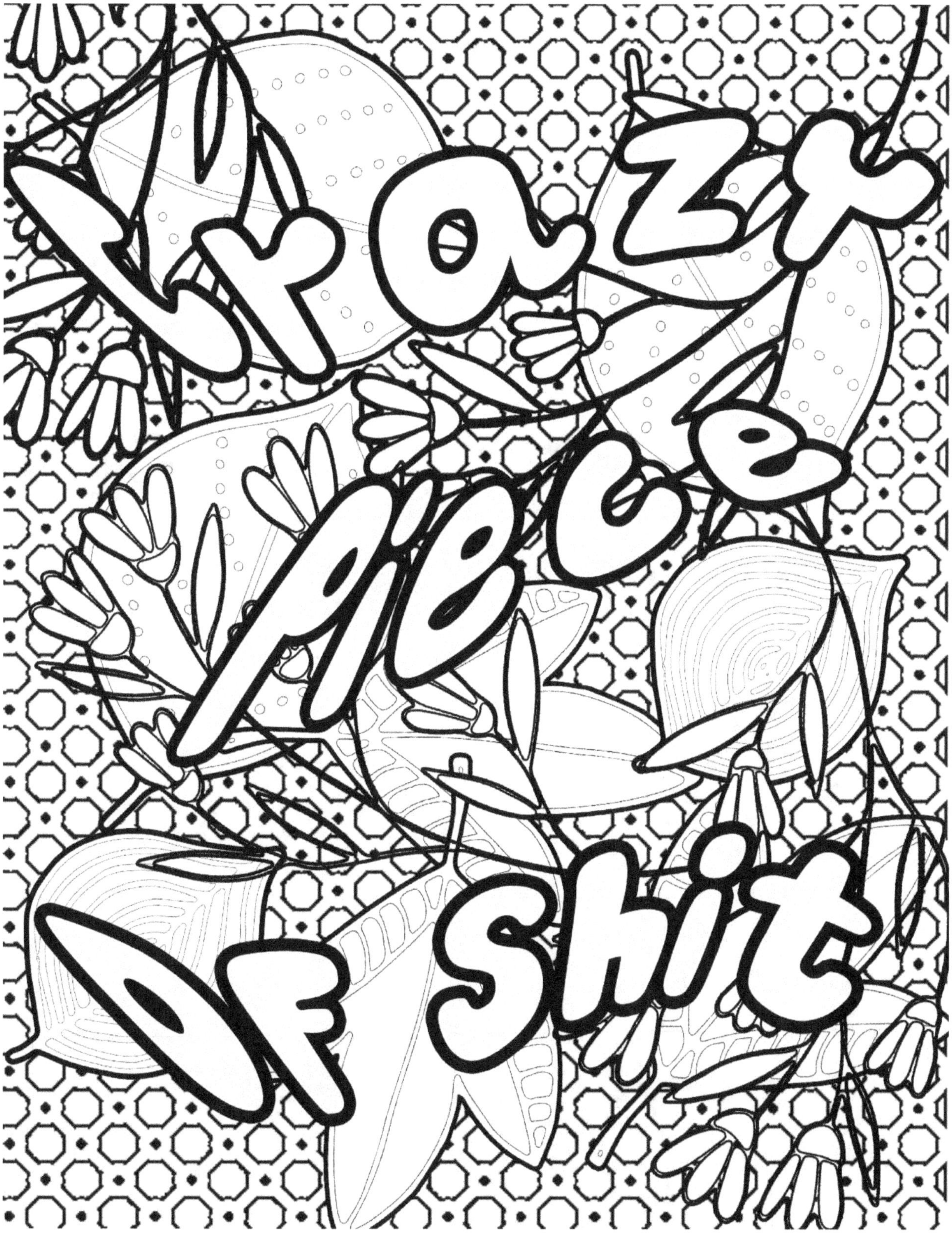
Crazy
piece
of shit

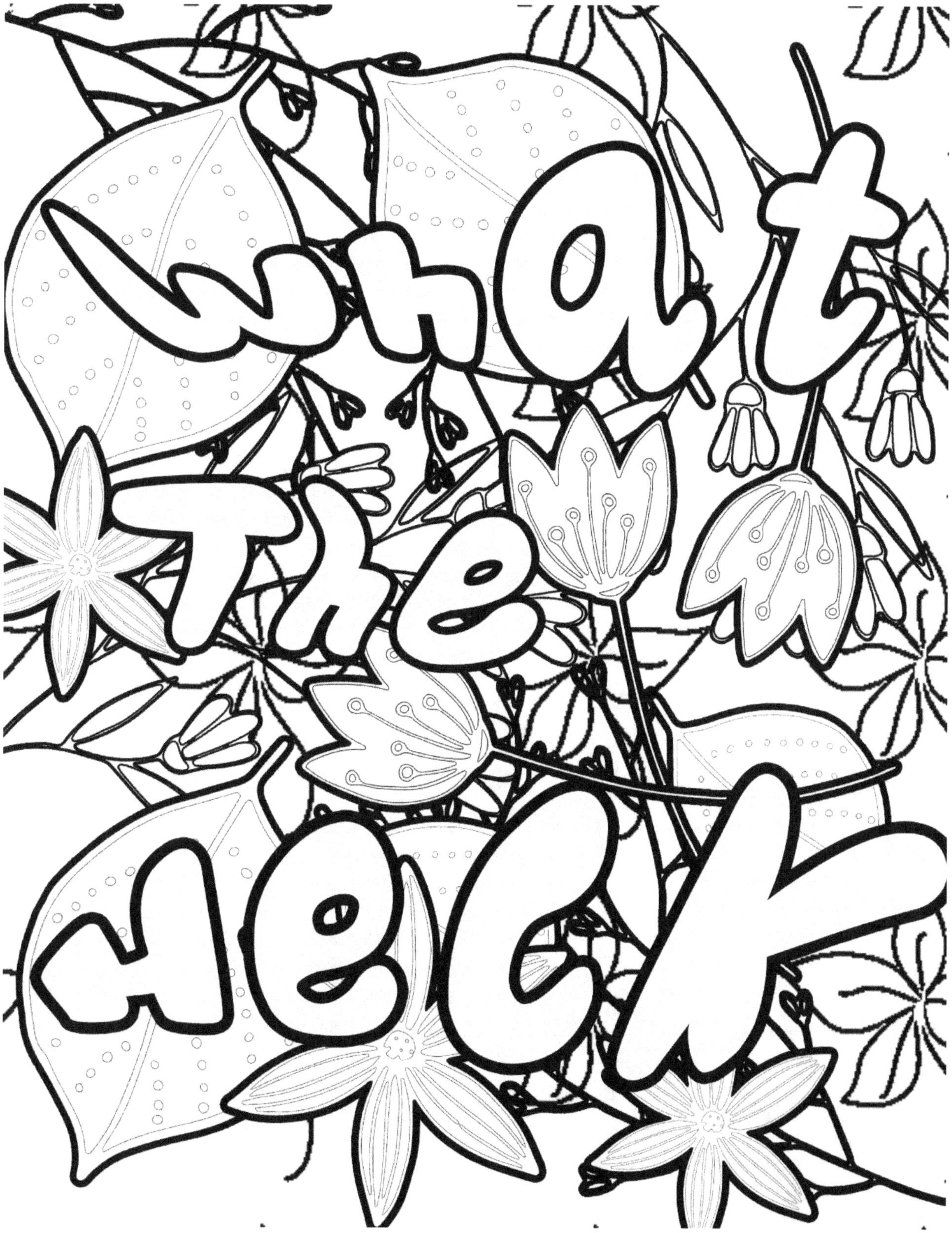
What
The
Heck

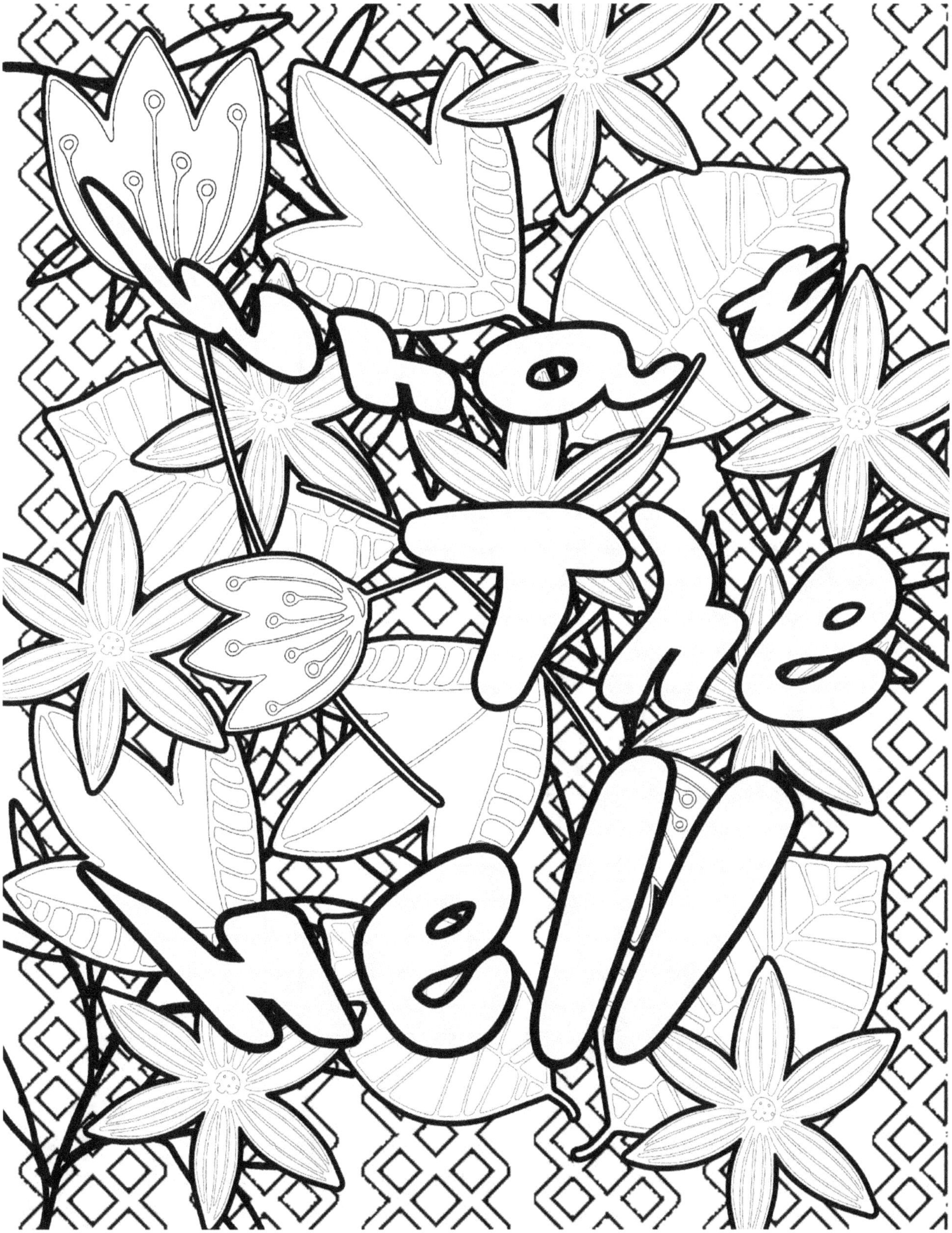
What The Hell

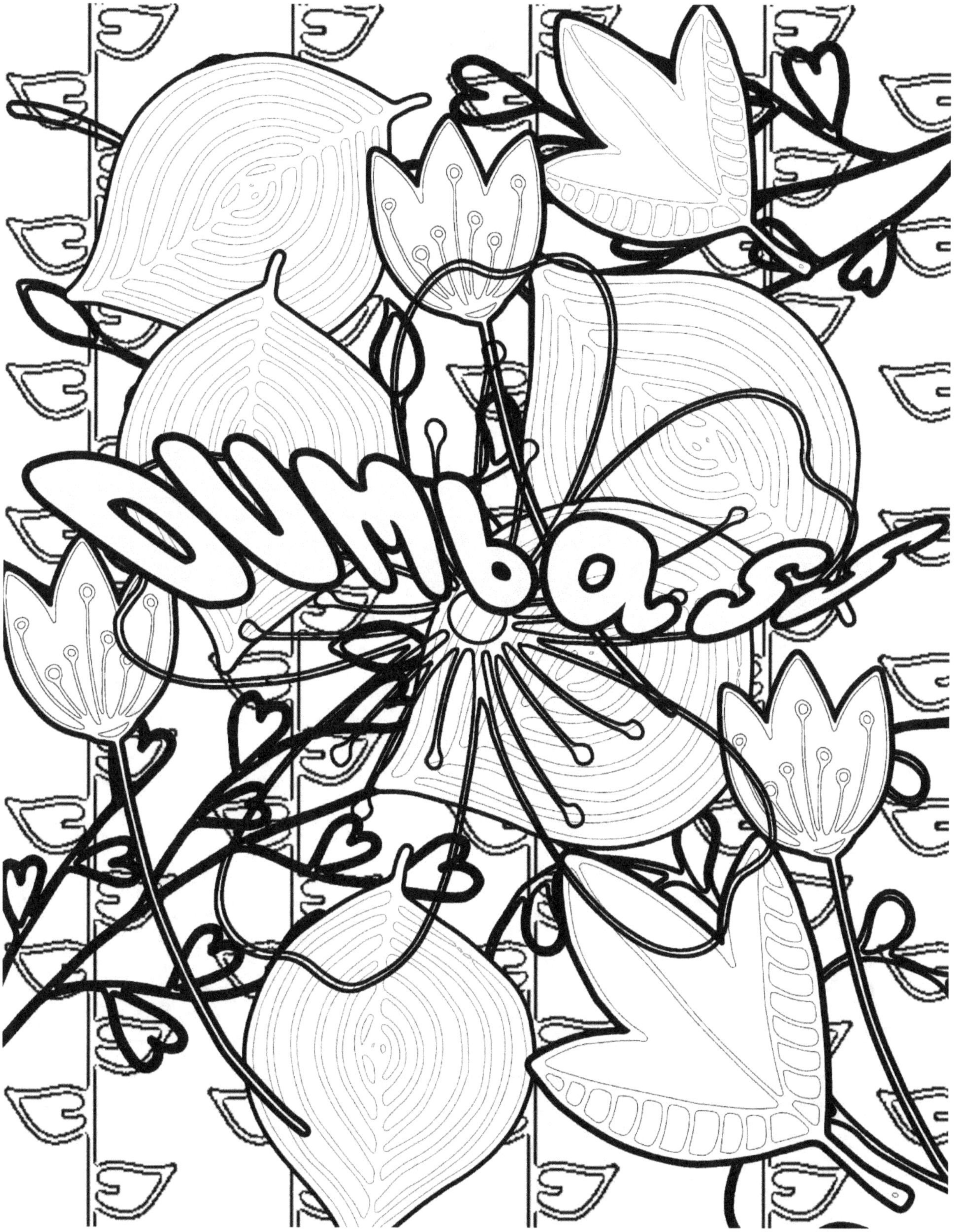
Dumbass!

Note

www.ingramcontent.com/pod-product-compliance
Lightning Source LLC
Chambersburg PA
CBHW081121180526
45170CB00008B/2951
9781539974987